Alvaro Maccioni

La Famiglia

THE COOKBOOK

Photography by David Loftus

PALAZZO

First published in 2011 by
PALAZZO EDITIONS LTD
2 Wood Street
Bath BA1 2JQ
www.palazzoeditions.com

Publisher: Colin Webb
Commissioned Photography: David Loftus
Art Director: Bernard Higton
Managing Editor: Judy Barratt
Recipe Editor: Gillian Haslam
Editorial Assistant: Stephanie Bramwell-Lawes

Typeset in Palatino, Coldstyle and Wiesbaden Swing.

ISBN: 978-0-9564942-3-8

A CIP catalogue record for this book is available from
the British Library.

Printed and bound in China by Imago.

10 9 8 7 6 5 4 3 2 1

A view across the olive groves towards Vinci,
where I was born.

1 Risotto FRAGOLE
2 Quello di cipolle
3 Medaglioni di vitello
4 Risotto di Porcini
5
(179) CANTUCCINI (Fichi secchi
Noci, Nocioline, Mandorle)

6 INSALATA ARANCI

7 Sbattivo di vitello
con Mascarpone

8 CODA di Rospo

Contents

Introduction

When people come to my cookery school, just outside the beautiful town of Lucca, in Tuscany, the first thing I ask them is if they have come to learn to cook Italian food. Inevitably, the eager heads nod enthusiastically. I smile, shake my head and say, 'Well, you may be disappointed. The only food you will learn to cook here is the food of Tuscany!' From its dialects to its cuisine, Italy is a deeply regional country. Even down to the shapes of the pasta, every part of Italy has its own preferences, its own identity, its own way to do things. When I opened my first restaurant, Alvaro's, in 1966 on London's King's Road, I brought to the UK – for the very first time – the real flavours of Tuscan food. My menu came straight from my family's table in Vinci, in the foothills of the Apennines. Every dish I put on the menu, I would have been equally happy to serve up at home, to my father, my mother, my grandparents and all my aunts and uncles. Every dish would have made them proud of me. This book is about my journey from that family table in a small village in Tuscany to London and La Famiglia, the restaurant that pays homage to my humble beginnings and celebrates those that are closest to us of all.

This is me (bottom row, far right) with the original staff from Alvaro's in 1966.

Food, family and festivals

When I was a child my life was punctuated by the call of food – from my mother, my grandmother and all the aunts and neighbours who used to feed my sister, friends and me every day. It was their passion for feeding us, their love of making something wonderful out of everything that grew in the gardens and on the forest floor around us, that I believe eventually gave me my own deep calling to *la cucina*.

Food unified my family. I grew up in the 1940s and we didn't have a television to gather around. Instead, recreation time was spent talking, laughing and even arguing. Most often, all that socializing happened around the kitchen table, as food came and went (and, for the adults, glasses of wine were poured and drunk dry). Often the conversation itself would centre around what we were eating. My mother, father and grandparents would talk about how easy or hard the food had been to find; they would discuss the cooking process and, usually, someone would make suggestions for improvement (these didn't always go down too well with the cook, of course!). On special occasions – when not only my immediate family, but also my extended family gathered to enjoy a meal together – the noise around the table would be deafening. I remember at one family meal, in Sanbaronto, my mother's home village, on 1 May (a feast day), forty-two members of my family sat at the same table, eating food cooked by all the mothers and grandmothers among us.

I loved those occasions, they epitomized my childhood and, now that I look back on them, I think they probably gave me my first insight into how food could lift the spirits of young and old and, most importantly, bring people together.

Quite often, major celebrations and festivals extended beyond blood family and involved the entire community. In Vinci, 8 September was the festival of St Joseph, when all the locals pooled their resources and food was made in one enormous camp, for everyone to enjoy. It was quite a spectacle! At *carnivale*, in February, with nothing else to do during the cold winter, every household would make some fantastic dish to bring to the celebration and then we'd all put on masks and join together for a huge street party. I particularly remember the smell of Florentine steak as it cooked on the communal bonfire on Epiphany (6 January); and of the barbecue gatherings that sprung up around the Apennine foothills on *ferr'agosto* (15 August, Italy's summer holiday day).

At the end of June, the wheat harvest began. Farmers and their farmhands would be out all day bringing home the harvest, while the wives and mothers of those hard-working men prepared a celebratory feast for their return. I remember those women laughing at me, telling me that I made a good tasting 'fork' as I tried everything that went out. My love of food had quite a reputation!

My mother was often absent from these celebrations. Although plenty of her favourite

These are the faces of my life — the family who gave me my love of food.

recipes appear in this book and on my menu even today, she was unwell for much of my childhood and spent long periods away from home in hospital. A boy growing up without the constant presence of his mother can be tough, but if there was a bright side to my predicament it was that I was able to gather rich and bountiful knowledge from all the kitchens around me. My grandparents and aunts would scoop up my sister and me from school and make sure we had good, healthy, hearty meals inside us. When they weren't available, our neighbours and friends would fight over who was to have us to lunch that day. They always made us feel like the guests of honour, with dishes of food fit for heroes. Sad as it was, my mother's illness enabled me to experience the cooking of all the people who surrounded me. The profound generosity of the friends who lived in those households gave me, I believe, a deep appreciation of what it meant to be open-hearted in spirit, to share, and to enjoy good company and good food no matter what the circumstances.

It wasn't until I'd been away from not only Vinci or Tuscany, but Italy altogether that I really learned to appreciate what my childhood experiences of family, extended family and community and food had taught me. When I arrived in Switzerland, eager to perfect my skills as a chef, I expected to learn more about food and flavour than anything I'd learned at home. In some respects I did – for example, I discovered how to serve food beautifully to make it look appetizing

and I learned to finesse my cooking techniques – but very few of the dishes I made there tasted anywhere near as good as the food I'd been given by all those wonderful people at home, the food that had come from the land and was tuned in to the seasons. I did my course and learned what I could in Switzerland, but then I went back to Vinci and rediscovered what real food tastes like. I knew then that I wanted to offer other people food from the kitchens of Tuscany, of Vinci. I went back to those households and I asked all the mothers, grandmothers, aunts, cousins and neighbours who had fed me so well as a boy to show me again my favourite dishes. I didn't at any time come across an unwilling teacher. I was welcomed into the kitchens then just as I had been as a boy.

The land is my larder

Even as children, my sister, cousins, friends and I would know what time of year it was by the dishes that arrived before us – lush, green vegetables and shiny, purple baby aubergines told us that it was spring; bright red, juicy tomatoes screamed that summer had arrived; mushrooms, beans and crunchy, juicy apples announced the arrival of autumn; while game, such as pheasant and wild boar, told us that winter was here and Christmas was coming. Every day, we ate what was growing in the garden or in the forests around our home. If the food hadn't been picked that day – as it often wasn't during winter – it had been collected and preserved by my *nonna* at other times of the year.

Having the land as our larder was particularly important during the Second World War. Rationing meant that food was scarce, but we learned quickly to identify which plants growing in the wild could supplement our staple diet. Chicory, rocket, chestnuts, mushrooms and an abundance of herbs were the obvious choices from the forests, but we also learned to identify more unusual delicacies. One of my particular favourites was the young green shoot of the blackberry bush, which tasted just like asparagus.

Meat came largely from the livestock on the land around us, too. We kept chickens (which provided us with eggs, as well as meat), pigs and cows in our own fields, while the countryside provided pigeon, rabbit and other game. There were no boundaries when it came to catching wild animals to eat. Game belonged to all of Italy, and as long as you were out to hunt, no farmer could chase you from his land.

During the war, once Italy had sided with the Allies, the German army would lead the cows off the farmland in Vinci to take them to the soldiers. This was hard – to watch livestock that we'd bred and reared for our own food taken away. One night, as the cows were being led down the road, I noticed that one had stopped to chew on a vine. Quietly, I tore the vine from the bush. I walked away from the herding cows, tempting the hungry cow to follow me by gently waving the vine behind my back. The cow followed me home to Vinci and I led it straight to a stable on our land.

Within two hours of my return, the local men had slaughtered it, skinned it and divided it up between the neighbours – everyone in the village would eat *manzo* (beef) that night! This story is important, because I was only eight years old, but this was the first time I had properly provided food for others. They treated me like a hero, but most importantly of all I felt like one!

When you come from a background of food that has roots embedded in the earth or a heart that's still beating almost until the moment it enters the cooking pot, it teaches you what true flavour is. The landscape of Tuscany provided me with my home, but its fertile soils provided me with a true understanding and appreciation of good food, and most importantly how the seasons make a profound difference to how food responds during cooking and to how it tastes. You can make a tomato sauce in winter, but the tomatoes you use won't be bright red and ripe and juicy. To create a rich sauce from unripe tomatoes requires cooking for twice or three times as long. That's why my grandmother would dry the last of the season's tomatoes on the vine, so that as the flavours intensified during the drying process, they would provide a good, tangy, flavourful tomato sauce for the winter months, when the best fresh tomatoes were long gone.

If you understand the land and the food it gives you, and you work with it, it will repay you a thousandfold in the flavours of the dishes you produce. In this book I've tried to bring you back

MR ALVARO

to nature, and to show you how to cook and eat with the seasons. Now that we can buy most ingredients at all times of the year, there's no need to eat only from, say, the summer chapter between July and September, or from the winter chapter when you've just seen in the new year, but I hope that dividing up the recipes by season will give you a sense of when most of the ingredients will be at their best, so that the aromas and flavours of your dishes will be at their most appetizing, too.

Beyond my Tuscan family

I left school early to earn money to supplement my father's income and to help out during the long periods of my mother's ill health. I worked in local bars and restaurants, and during the autumn did a little grape picking to earn extra cash. Eventually, I spent some time at agricultural college, but I knew that agriculture wasn't where my future lay and, by the time I was nearly eighteen, I had saved enough money to go to catering school in Lausanne, Switzerland, where I learned the techniques that would enable me to one day become a decent chef. When I got home, after collecting the wisdom of my friends, family and neighbours, serving the apprenticeships that were better than money could ever buy, I began working in some of Tuscany's best hotels, learning the trade that would eventually set me up for life.

Then, after two years travelling through France and Germany, all the time collecting what knowledge of the restaurant and hotel business I could, I arrived in England. I took a job as the sous chef at the Mirabelle hotel in London, then after a year or so joined the great Mario and Franco, owners of La Terrazza in Soho, where my passion for owning my own restaurant began. In 1966, I opened Alvaro's and I began my relationship with my restaurant family – all the chefs, sous chefs and front-of-house masters who would make my restaurant the amazing adventure, and success, it has been. By the time I opened La Famiglia in 1975, my wife Letizia and I had raised our own family (my sons Alessandro and Alfonso and my daughter Marietta) and I wanted the restaurant's name to always remind me what was important in my life, where I'd come from and how the best things in life are the people who are closest to us. La Famiglia is very much a family affair – even today, my daughter Marietta works with me at the restaurant. My sons, now in Australia and Brazil with their own families, always come home when it matters. In 2010, my wife and I celebrated our fiftieth wedding anniversary. What a party we had, with all my children and grandchildren gathered together, as well as my friends and the wonderful people who have made my life so colourful.

The members of staff at La Famiglia are like my extended family. How many other restaurant owners can say that their chef has been with them for almost forty years (thank you, Quinto!), or that their restaurant manager stayed with them from the day the restaurant opened until the day he retired (thank you, Gigi!)?

This book is my opportunity finally to gather together all the recipes that have made my family – old and new, related by circumstance as well as by blood – happy at my own Tuscan table. *La Famiglia: The Cookbook* contains not just the recipes that my mother, aunts, grandparents and neighbours taught me to make when I was little more than a child, but also those that I have assembled from my other major influences – my time in Switzerland, my friends from all around Italy, and especially my wife Letizia (who makes the best tomato sauce in the world!). This book is about celebrating the fact that good food comes from all the things that are natural to us – the land, the seasons and above all the family who help to create, prepare and enjoy it. I want the book to be my thank you to the spirit of giving and sharing that gave me my passion for cooking in the first place. Read, create, eat and like my grandchildren – the newest generation of my family – always come back for more.

Alvaro Maccioni

'This book is my opportunity finally to gather together all the recipes that have made my family — old and new, related by circumstance as well as by blood — happy at my own Tuscan table.'

Cooking like a Tuscan

I learned to cook by observation – my lessons in cookery were not from recipe books, and ingredients did not come with specific weights and measures. For me, cooking is an art – it's about the freshness of the ingredients and an instinct for what tastes good. This is why I want to encourage you to cook by the seasons, and also by your tastebuds. Following a few simple guidelines will help you achieve the best results.

• Use the quantities in the methods to guide you, but if you think a recipe needs a bit more or less of something, don't be afraid to experiment. A food's flavour will vary according to whether or not it's in season, so being prescriptive doesn't always reward you with the best results.

• Seasoning is a matter of taste. Sometimes I know that a recipe needs a good quantity of salt; sometimes just a pinch is enough. However, the amount of salt, pepper and other seasonings you use partly depends upon your own preferences. As you cook make sure you taste, taste, taste – then adjust the seasoning as you see fit.

• In my cooking, unless otherwise specified, I use sea salt, freshly ground black pepper, extra virgin olive oil, red wine vinegar, and dried red chilli. Table salt will do for boiling pasta or gnocchi (the salt simply encourages fast boiling). Sometimes the recipes call for 'best-quality extra virgin olive oil' when the flavour of the oil is really crucial to the dish – for these, use the best (preferably Tuscan) extra virgin olive oil you can find. At other times, standard extra virgin olive oil will work perfectly well. I only ever use Maccioni olive oil, from my family's own olive groves in Tuscany!

• Parmesan cheese is always freshly grated. I use Parmigiano Reggiano – authentic Parmesan cheese from Parma, northern Italy.

• Use locally sourced meat, poultry and fish from a reliable, reputable butcher or fishmonger. Free range poultry and meat, wild game, and non-farmed fish will always give you the best flavour.

• Unless otherwise specified, use medium-sized eggs, fruit and vegetables; fresh ingredients, including herbs; and level spoon measures. Throughout the book, I have used metric measures only. A conversion guide appears on page 232, as well as a guide to UK/US terms.

• Finally, many of the *primi piatti* recipes in this book call for freshly made pasta or gnocchi. To avoid repetition, the recipes for basic pasta and basic gnocchi appear over the page.

My chefs (previous page) are like my extended family. Quinto ha been with me for four decades!

Primavera
Spring

Tuscany in springtime fulfils all the romantic notions we might have of nature's reawakening following the cold of winter. From April to June the forest floor around Vinci becomes carpeted with wild primulas and bright blue violets. In the vineyards the buds

on the grapevines grow longer, while in the olive groves the leaves on the olive trees, which seem to stretch as far as the eye can see on every hill around the town, turn darker green. The foothills of the Apennines are lush and inviting, and on the days when the sun shines, the hillsides are bathed in a gentle, awakening light. As the last snow melts from the tops of the mountains, the days grow longer and all the plants, people and wildlife seem to wake up from their winter's rest.

When I was growing up, I remember the light in my mother's eyes as the garden started to come alive again. From our own land, we harvested an abundance of spring greens, such as spinach and kale. I remember shelling sweet, juicy garden peas with my *nonna* (eating a few straight from the pods, too, of course!) and I particularly remember the delicious asparagus and artichokes – and the most beautiful small aubergines. These were not big and bulbous like the ones we expect to see in the supermarket today, but small, juicy, firm and, by the latter half of spring, perfectly ripe.

I also think of this as a time of the most wonderful pasta. That might seem strange, given all the fresh vegetables that you normally associate with spring, but it was at this time of year that our chickens laid the most delicious eggs. The yolks were bright yellow and they were full of flavour. They also made fantastic *frittata*, a sort of Italian omelette.

The main festival of the season was, of course, Easter. The frugality of Lent was over (we gave up meat for Lent) and this was a time of abundance. We ate the freshest spring chickens, the tastiest rabbit, and lots of seafood – shellfish, freshwater fish, such as trout caught in the local rivers, and fish from the sea, caught in the Mediterranean and brought to shore by local fishermen.

In Vinci, we marked the end of spring with the festival of *San Pietro e San Paolo*, on 28 June. A church procession that involved the whole village was followed by a family meal. My mother or grandmother would arrive at the table with a mountain of the freshest egg pasta and then, to follow, a meat dish such as *Coniglio alla Contadina* (Farmhouse Rabbit; see p.59), served up with hunks of homemade bread. This was a special time for my family – a celebration of thanks for the new life that spring had given us and a welcome to the warm days of summer.

Melanzane all'Agrodolce
Aubergines in Sweet-and-sour Sauce

I have to confess that I was never a great lover of vegetables as a child, but my aunt Zia Tuilia knew that I always enjoyed her sweet-and-sour aubergines. She would make them for me as a light meal to have after school, layered up on crusty bruschetta. Today, the mixture makes a fantastic appetizer or delicious accompaniment at a buffet supper or a barbecue.

Serves 4–6

4 medium aubergines,
  cut into 1cm cubes
225ml extra virgin olive oil
2 celery sticks, sliced
2 onions, peeled and sliced
10 green olives, pitted and chopped
2 tbsp capers, drained
125ml tomato purée
125ml red wine vinegar
1 tbsp sugar
salt, to taste
2 tbsp pine nuts (optional), to serve

Sprinkle the aubergine cubes with salt and place them in a colander set over a plate to drain for 30 minutes.

Rinse and dry the aubergine cubes, then heat 175ml of the oil in a frying pan. Sauté the aubergine until crisp and well browned. Drain on kitchen paper and discard the used oil. Heat the remaining oil in the pan, add the celery and fry until golden and crisp, then remove using a slotted spoon and set aside. Using the same oil, repeat with the onion slices.

Once the onion is golden, return the aubergine and celery to the frying pan; stir in the olives, capers and tomato purée. Season with salt to taste. Allow the mixture to simmer in the frying pan for 10 minutes, then increase the heat, add the vinegar and sugar and stir until the vinegar has evaporated. Transfer to a serving dish, sprinkle with pine nuts, if using, and serve at room temperature.

Melanzane alla Parmigiana
Aubergine, Tomato and Cheese Bake

My mother used to make what seemed like mountains of this traditional dish when aubergines were in season, in late May and early June. Unlike today, when we can get most vegetables all the time, we didn't have aubergines at other times of year. As a child, I used to call the dish 'lasagne without pasta', because really that's exactly what it is!

Serves 6

3 medium aubergines, cut into slices 3mm thick

1.5kg tomatoes, peeled (see p.54)

125ml extra virgin olive oil, plus a little extra for oiling

500g Parmesan cheese, grated

20 basil leaves, torn into small pieces

salt and freshly ground black pepper, to taste

Preheat the grill to high and the oven to 180°C/Gas 4. Place the aubergine slices on the grill pan and brown both sides. Take care not to let the slices burn.

Place the tomatoes in a bowl and crush them with your hands (or pulse using a hand-held blender), stir in the oil, then season with the salt and freshly ground black pepper to taste (don't overdo the salt, as the Parmesan is already quite salty).

Oil a 20 x 30cm baking dish. Put some aubergine slices in the bottom of the dish, spoon some of the crushed tomatoes over, then sprinkle with Parmesan and some basil leaves – this is the first layer. Continue with successive layers until you have filled up the tray, or run out of ingredients (you'll need some Parmesan left for the topping) – I think that three or four layers are enough.

Cover the top layer with a generous sprinkling of Parmesan and place the dish in the preheated oven for 20 minutes. When cooked, allow the dish to rest for 10 minutes, then cut into portions (use a sharp knife, otherwise the layers will slide away from one another) and serve.

Salumi con Frittata
Platter of Salami with Italian Omelette

I think of this as a spring dish, because we always served it up on the feast of Ascension Day – the day that Christ rose to heaven following his resurrection on Easter Day. The only other time I remember it being made was when we had guests for Sunday lunch or supper, so it must have been special! My mother would place a huge dish in the middle of the table and everyone would tuck in while we were waiting for our pasta to arrive. Presented with chicken liver crostini (see p.138), it becomes a classic Tuscan antipasto. The dish is all about the presentation.

Serves 4

300g Italian cured meats, such as 100g Tuscan prosciutto, 100g mortadella and 100g Tuscan salami with fennel seeds (*finocchiona*)

3 eggs, beaten

extra virgin olive oil, for frying

5 basil leaves, torn

8 crostini slices

mixed vegetables in oil (optional)

salt and freshly ground black pepper, to taste

Arrange the cured meats equally on four serving plates. Season the beaten eggs with salt and freshly ground black pepper, and mix thoroughly. Heat a little oil in a small frying pan and use the beaten egg to make two *frittate*. Turn each *frittata* over to cook until golden on both sides. Take care not to fold the *frittate* as you remove them from the pan (Italian *frittata* is served open, not folded like a French omelette). As each *frittata* is cooked, sprinkle a little basil over. Cut each *frittata* in half and arrange one half next to the cured meats on each plate, along with two crostini (if you are making the crostini from scratch, for each one use a thick slice of ciabatta, brushed with a little olive oil and then placed under a hot grill until toasted). If you're using the mixed vegetables with oil, place one or two heaped tablespoons on each plate. You can serve the *frittate* hot or cold.

Variation: If you are feeling adventurous, try putting the cured meats through a mincer and mixing them into the beaten egg before frying – this will make little salami *frittatine*, which you can serve simply sprinkled with basil and with a few crostini on the side.

Mousse di Ricotta Salata al Basilico
Ricotta and Basil Mousse

My grandmother from my mother's side always kept sheep, so I was raised on the freshest, most delicious ricotta I think I've ever known. Until my *nonna* made this dish for me, I couldn't understand how ricotta could be eaten without sugar to take away the bitter edge. I loved her mousse so much — it was a treat, as sweet and as special as cake.

Serves 4

225g ricotta cheese

150ml homemade yogurt
  or natural Greek yogurt

5 tbsp chicken stock

1 garlic clove, peeled

1 tbsp chopped basil,
  plus 12 whole leaves

2 tbsp pine nuts, chopped

3 tsp powdered gelatine

1 tsp green peppercorns

salt and freshly ground black pepper,
  to taste

tomato sauce (see p.51), to serve

Grease and line a 450g loaf tin or terrine with non-stick silicone or greaseproof paper, rubbed with a little oil (soak a kitchen towel in oil and rub it all over the paper or silicone).

Put the ricotta cheese, yogurt, stock, garlic and chopped basil into a liquidizer or food processor; blend until smooth. Mix in the pine nuts and add salt and pepper to taste.

Put the gelatine into a small heatproof bowl with 2 tbsp water and leave to stand for 1 minute, then place the bowl in a pan of hot water (off the heat) and leave until the gelatine has dissolved, about 2 minutes. Stir the dissolved gelatine into the cheese mixture. Leave on one side for a few minutes until it starts to thicken – you'll know it's thick enough when it coats the back of a spoon. Stir the green peppercorns into the mousse mixture.

Spoon half the mixture into the prepared tin and lay the whole basil leaves over the top. Finish off with the remaining mousse mixture, spreading the surface level with a knife. Chill for 4 hours or until firm enough to slice.

To serve, turn the mousse out and cut into slices 1cm thick. Place a little tomato sauce on each plate and top with a slice of mousse.

Variation: Try using watercress in place of basil; use 2 tbsp coarsely chopped watercress in the mousse mixture, and lay several large watercress leaves through the middle of the mousse.

Cook's tip: After the gelatine has been added to the mousse mixture, try putting the mixture in the freezer for a minute or two, in order for the mousse to thicken more quickly.

Carciofini Fritti

Fried Baby Artichokes

People think that this dish is made using the first artichokes of the season, but actually when the fully grown artichokes are cut from the stalk, there remains a little shoot, and this is what we used at home. In Italy we call these little shoots 'blue', because they are sky blue in colour. Surprisingly, they aren't bitter, but beautifully sweet.

Serves 4

10 small artichokes
juice of 1 lemon
extra virgin olive oil, for deep frying
2 eggs, beaten
plain flour, for coating
salt and freshly ground black pepper,
  to taste

Remove and discard all the hard exterior leaves of the artichokes and cut off the sharp points, so that you end up with a stalk approximately 2.5cm long, the heart and three-quarters of the tender leaves.

Add the lemon juice to a basin of cold water, then slice the artichoke into thin strips and put these into the basin, too. Leave the artichoke strips to soak for 30 minutes (the lemon juice will prevent them from discolouring), then drain and dry them thoroughly on kitchen paper.

Heat the oil in a deep frying pan until very hot (a cube of day-old bread should brown in it in less than a minute).

Season the beaten eggs. Toss the artichoke slices in the flour and dip into the beaten egg. When they are well coated, fry them until golden and crisp. Do this in batches, if necessary, and reheat the oil between each batch. Keep the cooked artichoke strips in a warming oven while you cook the rest. Drain the fried artichokes on kitchen paper and serve as soon as possible.

Cook's tip: To clean and prepare an artichoke, remove the bendable outer leaves until you come to leaves that, as you try to bend them, snap in two. These are the young, edible leaves.

Crostata di Asparagi in Bellavista
Fresh Asparagus Tart

One of my aunts lived in France for a while and it was she who brought this dish to our home. The tart is like a quiche, which for me as a child was something completely strange and different. With its distinct flavour, asparagus was far from my favourite vegetable and this was the only way anyone could convince me to eat it.

Serves 6

200g plain flour

100g butter or margarine, cut into small pieces, plus extra for greasing

3 eggs

a pinch of nutmeg

100ml whole milk

50g Parmesan cheese, grated

100g Emmental cheese, grated

500g asparagus (fresh or frozen), boiled until *al dente*

1 hard-boiled egg, shelled and sliced

salt, to taste

To make the pastry casing, arrange the flour in a pile on a worktop and place the butter in the centre. Slowly work the ingredients together with your fingertips, then add one whole egg, a pinch of salt and 4–5 tablespoons of water. Continue working the mixture with your fingertips until the pastry comes together into a ball. If the dough is too sticky, add a little more flour.

Preheat the oven to 200°C/Gas 6. Butter a 25cm round baking tin. Roll out the pastry and line the tin. Place some baking beans or dry beans on the pastry (to prevent the pastry browning too quickly or drying out). Bake in the preheated oven for 15 minutes.

Meanwhile, to make the tart filling, in a bowl beat the two remaining eggs with a pinch of salt, the nutmeg and milk and both grated cheeses.

Remove the pastry case from the oven, discard the beans and pour the egg mixture over the pastry. Arrange the asparagus on the top, like spokes radiating out from the centre. Return the tart to the oven for a further 10 minutes, then remove it from the oven, decorate it with the hard-boiled egg slices and serve.

Cook's tip: If you're worried about your pastry sticking to the tin, line it with baking parchment or greaseproof paper first.

Carciofi Sott'Olio
Artichokes Preserved in Oil

During springtime, the Tuscan artichoke harvest is often abundant. When my mother's crop was so plentiful that we had too many to eat, we would blanche them and then put them *sott'olio* – in olive oil – to preserve them so that we could eat artichokes out of season, too.

Serves 6

12 small globe artichokes
  (morellini, if available)
juice of 2 lemons
500ml white wine
60ml red wine vinegar
10 bay leaves
whole black peppercorns
best-quality extra virgin olive oil

Carefully clean the artichokes, remove the hard exterior leaves and trim the stalks and the tops, and then place the hearts in a saucepan of water with the lemon juice. Put the saucepan on the heat, adding the white wine, vinegar, 2 bay leaves and 10 black peppercorns. Boil gently until the artichokes are *al dente* (about 6–10 minutes, depending on the size of the artichokes). When cooked, the artichokes must still be crisp.

Drain well, leaving the artichokes upside down to cool on a tea towel. Place the cooled artichokes to dry in the refrigerator (for a whole day if necessary), leaving them upside down on one clean tea towel and covered with another. When you're ready, layer the artichokes in sterilized jars (boil the jars in water for 5 minutes to sterilize them), alternating each layer with the remaining bay leaves and a few peppercorns. Cover with olive oil and seal the jars tightly. Store the artichokes for 2–3 months like this in a cool, dark place. For a longer shelf life, seal the jar tightly, then put the sealed jar in a pan of boiling water for another 10 minutes. This will create a vacuum inside the jar, which will preserve the artichokes, unopened, for up to one year.

Variation: If you wish, crumble a dried red chilli pepper or add a pinch (and I mean just a pinch!) of fennel seeds into the jar.

Cook's tip: Any vegetable can be preserved in exactly the same way as the artichokes.

Linguine alle Vongole Veraci
Linguine with Clams

My mother had a 'golden touch' when it came to cooking seafood! All her seafood dishes were beautiful. When May arrived we would make our first trip to Viareggio to buy fresh clams and bring them back for her to clean and cook at home. This dish is a special family favourite.

Serves 4

extra virgin olive oil
1 garlic clove, peeled and chopped
1 dried red chilli pepper
400g clams, scrubbed clean
1 glass white wine
400g linguine
salt, to taste
chopped parsley, to serve

Heat some oil in a frying pan (preferably one that has a lid), add the garlic and crumble in the chilli. Fry over a high heat until the garlic is golden. Add the clams and cook, covered, on a low heat until the clam shells open, about 10 minutes. Discard any clams that do not open. Pour in the glass of white wine and continue to cook, covered, on a low heat for a further 10 minutes.

Cook the linguine in a pan of salted boiling water until *al dente*. Once the pasta is ready, drain it, return it to the pan and add the clams and cooking liquor. Toss the pasta and sauce together, sprinkle with some chopped parsley and serve.

Tagliolini con Gamberi
Tagliolini with Prawn Sauce

This was a family favourite for special occasions, such as when we were celebrating birthdays or *onomastici* (saint days), or when important friends came for lunch. The light sauce makes it perfect for springtime – I remember eating it outdoors on the first warm days of the year.

Serves 4

50g onions, peeled and finely chopped

30g celery, finely chopped

12 prawns, peeled, and deveined if necessary, shells retained

5 garlic cloves, peeled and finely chopped

3 sprigs parsley

1/2 bay leaf

200ml white wine

120g tomatoes, roughly chopped

30g shallots, peeled and finely chopped

1/2 tbsp butter

30ml extra virgin olive oil

1 sprig thyme

300g fresh tagliolini

salt and freshly ground black pepper, to taste

1 sprig basil, to serve

To make the sauce, place the onion and celery in a saucepan with the prawn shells and four-fifths of the garlic, and the parsley and torn bay leaf. Season with pepper and add just enough water to cover all the ingredients. Bring to a gentle boil and cook, uncovered, for 30 minutes. From time to time skim away any impurities that appear on the surface. Strain the liquid into another saucepan, add the white wine and return the stock to the heat. Simmer until the liquid has reduced by half.

Place the tomato pieces in a frying pan (no need to add any oil) and heat gently until they release their own juice. Drain off any juice that has accumulated in the pan. Meanwhile, in another frying pan, sweat the shallots and remaining garlic until soft, then add the butter. Add the cooked tomatoes and continue to heat gently.

Reheat the prawn sauce and check the seasoning. Heat the olive oil in another pan, add the prawns and thyme and fry for approximately 1 minute, then keep warm.

Cook the tagliolini in a pan of lightly salted boiling water. Drain the pasta, mix with the tomatoes, prawns and sauce. Add the sprig of basil and a sprinkle of olive oil, and serve.

Variation: If you prefer, you can use 120g chanterelle mushrooms in place of the tomatoes and sprinkle with a tablespoon of chopped chives, rather than using a sprig of basil, at the end.

Gnudi di Ricotta e Ortiche
Naked Ricotta and Nettle Gnocchi

Originating from my home village of Vinci, this dish is a kind of pasta ... without the pasta! The 'naked' gnocchi are like ravioli fillings without the pasta casing. Light and delicate, *gnudi* were made in my family only for important feasts and celebrations, such as Easter. When they arrived on the table, even as children we knew that this was a special day.

Serves 6

For the gnocchi
500g ricotta
300g nettle sprouts, or spinach
4 eggs
100g Parmesan cheese, grated
1/4 tsp nutmeg
2 handfuls of flour, for dusting
salt and freshly ground black pepper,
    to taste

For the sauce
extra virgin olive oil
1 onion, peeled and finely chopped
12 courgette or marrow flowers, washed
    and dried
185ml whole milk
1 tsp pine nuts
salt, to taste

In a bowl, thoroughly mix together all the ingredients for the gnocchi, except the flour. Shape the mixture into balls the size of small golf balls (see tip, below), then dust with the flour.

To make the sauce, heat some oil in a frying pan and sauté the onion until soft, add the flowers and, after a few minutes, the milk and pine nuts. Stir once. Once the sauce has acquired a creamy consistency, remove the pan from the heat and whisk the sauce.

Cook the gnocchi in a pan of salted boiling water. Once cooked (they will be ready when they rise to the surface of the water), drain, season and mix with the sauce.

Cook's tip: To make perfectly shaped gnocchi, take a wine glass and flour the inside. Put half a tablespoon of gnocchi mixture into the floured glass and swirl the base of the glass round and round on your work surface until the mixture makes a perfect ball. Repeat until you've used all the gnocchi mixture.

Testaroli al'Alio e Basilico
Testaroli with Garlic and Basil Sauce

Typical of the Lunigiana region of Tuscany, this dish uses the first shoots of basil at the end of April to make a sauce similar to pesto, but lighter and more delicate. Its preparation requires a *testo* – a flameproof casserole with a lid, which is placed directly on charcoal. You can make the dish using fresh tagliatelle if you don't have time to make the *testaroli*.

Serves 3

250g wheat flour (type '00')

1 handful of basil leaves, finely chopped

2 tbsp grated pecorino cheese, plus extra to serve

1 garlic clove, peeled, cored and roughly chopped (see tip, below)

extra virgin olive oil

salt, to taste

Place the flour in a bowl, add a pinch of salt and add water little by little to make a batter with the consistency of double cream. Pour the batter into the casserole and cover it with the lid. Place the casserole directly on the charcoal (the coals should be very hot).

After 5 minutes check the consistency of the batter: it should have the appearance of a homogenous wafer with a number of little holes in the surface, caused by the water evaporating. Remove the batter from the casserole, transfer it to a plate, cover it with a clean tea towel and leave it to cool.

While the batter is cooling down, prepare the basil sauce. Mix the basil with the cheese and the garlic. Using a pestle and mortar, pound the mixture until it is compact, then transfer it to a cup and dilute it with a drizzle of olive oil until you have the required consistency – it should be like a thick sauce that falls off a spoon.

Bring a pan of salted water to the boil. Cut the *testaroli* batter in lozenge shapes approximately 7.5cm long. Tip the shapes into the boiling water. If the batter is fresh, it will take approximately 1 minute for the *testaroli* to cook. Drain the shapes and transfer them to individual plates, placing them in layers. Dress with the pesto sauce and additional pecorino cheese.

Cook's tip: Discarding the internal 'core' of the garlic cloves makes garlic easier for your body to digest. Look carefully at each clove and cut out the slightly darker part on the inside edge.

Garganelli alle Verdure
Garganelli with Vegetables

When the first shoots of vegetables arrived in spring, my sister Liana, even at the tender age of sixteen, would turn her hand to this wonderfully fresh pasta dish. Her version was always the best – and no wonder! She would take herself around the local gardens seeking out the freshest ingredients from our neighbours. This recipe uses carrots, peas and green beans, but you can choose any spring vegetables that are in season – it's also delicious with courgettes and celery.

Serves 4

4 tbsp extra virgin olive oil

50g carrot, peeled and cut into strips

50g onion, peeled and diced

40g green beans, chopped

4 tbsp fresh peas, or frozen if fresh are unavailable

200g tomatoes

2 sprigs marjoram

320g fresh garganelli pasta

a few basil leaves, to decorate

salt and white pepper, to taste

Heat half the olive oil in a casserole, add the carrots and onion and sauté over a low heat until the onions are soft. After a few minutes, add the green beans and peas and salt and pepper to taste; keep moist by adding a little water. Cook until the beans are *al dente*.

Using a slotted spoon, place the tomatoes in a large bowl of boiling water. Leave them for 1 minute, then drain and peel them (see p.54). Halve them, discard the seeds, chop the flesh into cubes and mix with the other ingredients in the casserole. Continue cooking, uncovered, for about 10 minutes, then add the marjoram and the remaining oil.

Meanwhile, cook the garganelli in a pan of boiling salted water until *al dente* (it's virtually impossible to overcook garganelli). Drain the pasta, add it to the casserole with the vegetables and toss everything together to incorporate all the sauce. Season and serve decorated with a few leaves of basil and a drizzle of olive oil.

Risotto ai Frutti di Mare
Seafood Risotto

When I was a boy, even though we didn't have fast cars like we have now, getting to the seaside would take only about half an hour. These days, the same journey takes three times that long because of the traffic! Trips to the seaside always involved coming back with bags full of fresh seafood, which my mother would turn into the most spectacular seafood risotto.

Serves 4

10 mussels
10 clams
50g unsalted butter
1/2 onion, peeled and finely chopped
1 celery stick, finely chopped
1/2 carrot, peeled and finely chopped
140g squid, skin on, chopped
300g Arborio rice
2 litres fish stock, kept simmering
10 medium prawns, unshelled
150g Parmesan cheese, grated

Bring a pan of water to the boil, add the mussels and the clams and boil until they open up. Drain and set aside. (Do not force any of the shells open; if they remain closed, this means that the fish is not edible and should be discarded.)

Melt the butter in a casserole, add the onion, celery and carrot and fry until the onion is soft and translucent. Add the chopped squid, stir and cook for 2 minutes over a gentle heat. Add the rice, and a ladle of stock and continue stirring, gradually adding more fish stock as the rice absorbs it (the risotto will take about 20 minutes to cook).

After 10 minutes, add the unshelled prawns, and the cooked mussels and clams. Stir continuously to prevent the rice sticking to the pan. In the last 5 minutes of cooking, stir in the grated Parmesan cheese. When the rice is cooked, remove the pan from the heat and allow the risotto to rest for 5 minutes before serving.

Risotto al Nero di Seppie
Risotto with Cuttlefish Ink

Every year we waited until March, when cuttlefish (a seafood relative of the squid) was at the best price at market, to enjoy this dish. We always knew it was spring when cuttlefish appeared on the table.

Serves 4–6

750g cuttlefish with ink sacs

1.2 litres fish stock, kept simmering

3 tbsp extra virgin olive oil

1/2 onion, peeled and finely chopped

2 garlic cloves, peeled and chopped

500g risotto rice, preferably
  Vialone Nano Gigante

125ml dry white wine

1 tbsp unsalted butter

3 tbsp finely chopped flatleaf parsley

salt and freshly ground black pepper,
  to taste

Rinse the cuttlefish in cold water and remove the tentacles and heads. Carefully remove the ink sacs from the heads without splitting the sacs.

Put the ink sacs in a strainer set over a small bowl and, using the back of a teaspoon, press out the ink. Pour a few tablespoons of the fish stock over the sacs, and extract the rest of the ink by allowing it to drain away with the stock. Prepare the cuttlefish by removing all the internal organs and the backbone. Wash thoroughly and cut the flesh into thin rings and strips.

Heat the oil in a large saucepan, add the onion and garlic and fry gently until translucent and soft, but not brown. Add the cuttlefish and cook gently for about 20 minutes until tender, adding a little stock to the pan if necessary during cooking. Add all the rice and stir thoroughly. When the grains are lightly toasted, add the wine and the ink and stir together until hot.

Continue cooking by adding the hot stock, one ladleful at a time. Keep stirring and always allow the liquid to be absorbed before adding any more. Also, remember to scrape down the side of the saucepan carefully. As soon as the risotto is cooked (this will take 18–20 minutes), remove the pan from the heat and stir in the butter, parsley, salt and pepper. Cover and leave to rest for approximately 3 minutes, then stir again and place on a warmed platter to serve.

Risotto ai Gamberi e Carciofi
Prawn and Artichoke Risotto

Arduina, a much-loved family friend who lived in our village, would cook us this dish, which she learned in the hotel kitchens of Montecatini, where she worked during the summer tourist season. She was a wonderful cook and this dish felt very sophisticated to us all.

Serves 4

80ml extra virgin olive oil

1 garlic clove, peeled and chopped

3 artichokes, tough outer leaves removed
 and chopped

300g prawns, shelled and deveined

400g Arborio rice

1 glass white wine

1.5 litres fish stock

2 tbsp finely chopped flatleaf parsley,
 plus a few whole leaves to serve

80g butter

salt and freshly ground black pepper,
 to taste

Heat the oil in a large frying pan, add the garlic, artichokes and prawns and lightly fry. Add the rice and white wine, allowing the wine to evaporate slowly. Add a ladle of fish stock and season, then continue to add stock a ladle at a time, stirring constantly – allow each addition of stock to be absorbed before adding more. Continue this process until the rice is cooked but still firm to the bite.

Stir in the chopped parsley and butter. Serve on a hot plate and decorate by placing whole parsley leaves in the centre.

Timballo di Riso
Rice Timbale

My father loved to eat rice, so as a family we ate a lot of traditional Tuscan rice dishes such as *timballo di riso*. Thankfully, anything my mother made with rice was always delicious.

Serves 6

For the crust

1 tbsp coarse salt

1 garlic clove

360g Arborio rice

juice of 1 lemon

5 extra-large eggs, beaten

90g Parmesan cheese, grated

a pinch of grated nutmeg

a pinch of ground cinnamon

5 tbsp capers preserved in vinegar, drained

1 tbsp unsalted butter, for greasing

15g breadcrumbs (preferably homemade)

salt and freshly ground black pepper, to taste

For the stuffing

2kg Swiss chard or spinach

6 tbsp extra virgin olive oil

4 carrots, peeled and finely chopped

3 celery sticks, finely chopped

2 red onions, peeled and finely chopped

1 garlic clove, peeled and finely chopped

10 sprigs flatleaf parsley, finely chopped

5 basil leaves, finely chopped, plus a few extra whole leaves to garnish

3 squabs (young pigeons), cleaned and dried with kitchen paper (use poussin or quail if you can't find squab)

500g very ripe fresh tomatoes (or tinned plum tomatoes)

500ml lukewarm beef or chicken stock

salt and freshly ground black pepper, to taste

To make the rice crust, bring a large pan of water to the boil, add the salt, garlic and rice. Stir and simmer, uncovered, for 8 minutes. Drain the rice under cold running water and transfer it to a china or glass container. Discard the clove, add the lemon juice and mix. Cover the container and let the rice stand while you prepare the stuffing.

Soak the Swiss chard in a bowl of cold water for 30 minutes – this will soften the stalks so that they cook in the same time as the leaves. Bring a large pan of water to the boil, salt to taste, then add the chard and boil for 5 minutes. Drain and cool the chard under cold running water. Lightly squeeze it to remove excess water, then coarsely chop.

Warm the oil in a large casserole over a medium heat. Add the chopped vegetables, garlic and herbs and sauté for 10 minutes. Add the whole squabs and sauté on all sides for a further 15 minutes. Add the tomatoes, cover and cook for 40 minutes, turning the squabs several times. Keep the squabs moist by adding stock as needed. Once the squabs are cooked and the sauce is quite thick, remove the casserole from the heat and transfer the squabs to a board.

Using a sharp knife, separate the meat from the bones and discard the latter. Replace the meat in the casserole (keep it in large pieces). Place the casserole over a medium heat for 10 minutes. Season with salt and pepper, then transfer the mixture from the casserole to a china or glass bowl and let it stand for about 30 minutes until cool.

Preheat the oven to 200°C/Gas 6. Remove 240ml of the squab sauce and pour it on to the cold rice. Add the eggs and Parmesan and season with salt, pepper, nutmeg and cinnamon. Add the capers and mix all the ingredients together with a wooden spoon.

Butter a 25cm casserole and line it with breadcrumbs. Save the leftover breadcrumbs. Line the casserole with two-thirds of the rice mixture. Cover with two-thirds of the boiled Swiss chard and place the squab pieces and sauce in the centre. Make a layer of the remaining Swiss chard, then a layer of the remaining rice. Sprinkle the leftover breadcrumbs over the rice and bake for 35 minutes.

Remove the timbale from the oven and let it cool for a few minutes, then carefully turn it out on to a large, round serving dish. Garnish with basil leaves. Serve immediately, sliced like cake.

Pomarola
Tomato Sauce

The first fleshy, ripe tomatoes of the season arrive in May, as the days start to become consistently warmer. In Tuscany we make tomato sauce by cooking our tomatoes in a frying pan; but in Sicily, where my wife Letizia comes from, they are boiled with garlic, onions, carrot and celery and strained to make this rich and fruity sauce. I'd like to say that my family love my version best, but it wouldn't be true – when my grandchildren, who live all over the world, come to visit, the first thing they ask for is always Nonna Letizia's delicious *pomarola*!

Makes 6–10 servings

2kg ripe tomatoes, roughly chopped
2 onions, peeled and chopped
1 carrot, peeled and chopped
2 celery sticks, chopped
extra virgin olive oil
salt, to taste

Place all the chopped vegetables in a large saucepan. Heat slowly to boiling point over a moderate heat. Periodically skim off the excess juices with a ladle (how often you need to do this will depend on the quality and ripeness of the tomatoes), leaving only the red, juicy pulp of the tomatoes to cook along with the other vegetables. When the mixture has broken up, lower the heat and drizzle a thin stream of oil into the pan, adding a pinch of salt. Cover, and continue cooking for 10 minutes, then remove the lid and cook for a further 10 minutes.

Remove the pan from the heat and leave to cool a little, then pass the sauce through a vegetable mill. Allow to cool completely and pour into sterilized, airtight jars. (Sterilize the jars by placing them, empty, in a pan of boiling water for 5 minutes.)

Drizzle a little olive oil on top of the sauce in each jar, then seal the jar and place in a pan of boiling water for 10 minutes. Cool completely and store, unopened, for up to 6 months. Once opened, the sauce will keep in a cool, dark place or fridge for 8–10 days.

Cook's tip: I prefer to use 'Florentine' tomatoes (that is, those tubby, rather ungainly ones that are a bit like apples or miniature pumpkins in shape) to make this sauce. They are rich in juicy pulp and sweet to taste, even more so than the Neapolitan plum tomatoes, which are all smooth and roughly olive-shaped. If you don't live in Florence, though, you will probably have to find something else suitable to replace my adored *fiorentini*.

Whichever tomatoes you use, try adding a sprig or two of basil (if it's in season) during the cooking stage. Then, if you're preserving the sauce, add a few whole, fresh basil leaves to each jar so that, when you eat the sauce during the winter months, the aromas remind you of warmer, sunnier days.

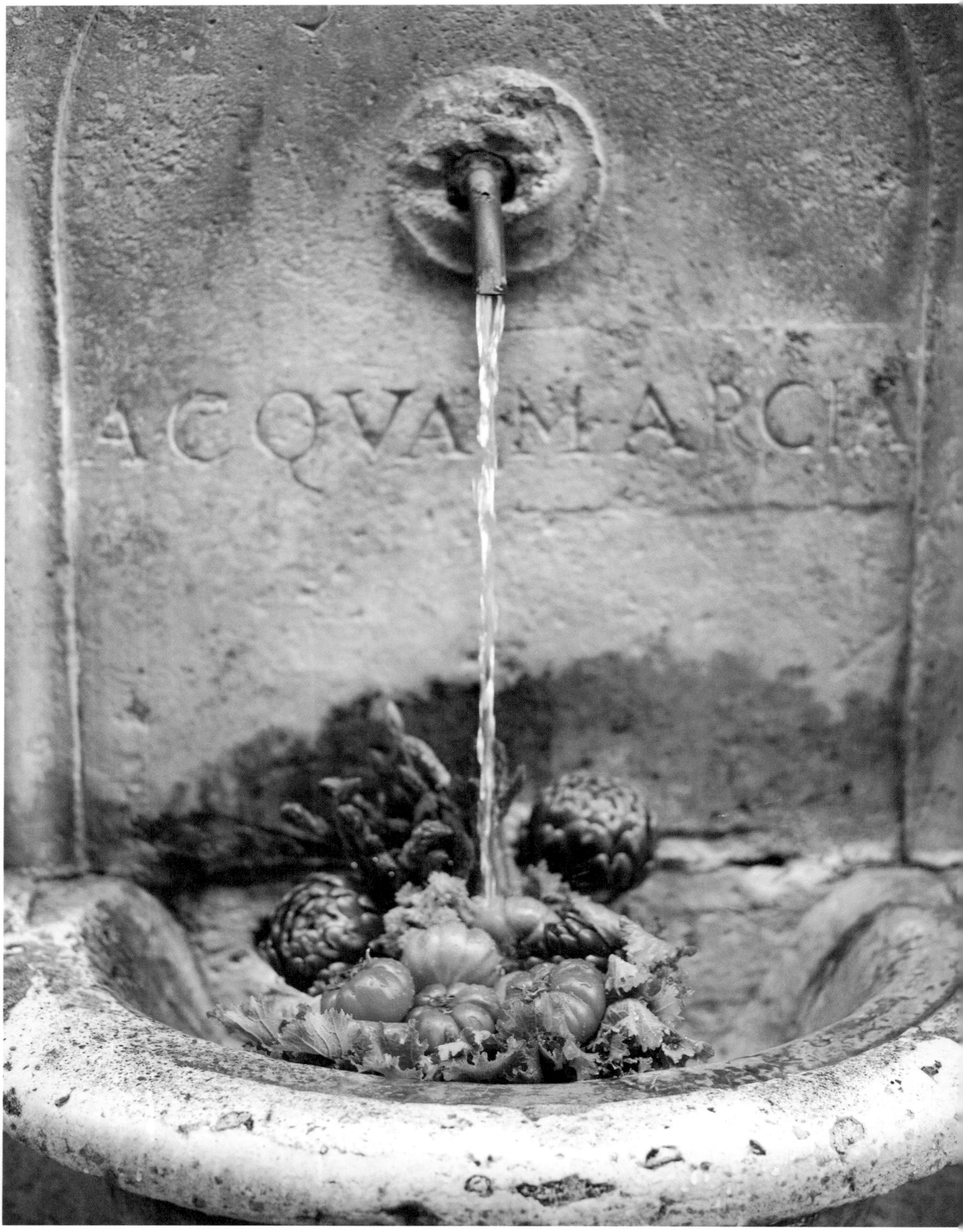
ACQVA MARCI

Salsa d'Aragosta
Lobster Sauce

I learned to make this dish at catering school in Lausanne, Switzerland, and it soon became one of my favourites. It has a place close to my heart – it was the first dish I ever made using lobster and the first shellfish dish that I had ever made on my own, without the help of a teacher. Even today it appears on my menu at La Famiglia.

Serves 8

4 live lobsters
6 tbsp extra virgin olive oil
4 garlic cloves, peeled and crushed
250ml white wine
150g tomatoes, peeled (see below)
250ml fish stock
1 dried red chilli pepper
salt and freshly ground black pepper,
   to taste

Split the lobsters in two and press with a meat flattener. Alternatively, if you wish to kill the lobsters beforehand, or don't fancy killing them by splitting them in two, you can put them in the freezer for an hour before you begin making the dish.

Heat the olive oil in a casserole over a high heat and add the crushed garlic cloves. Once the garlic has browned a little, add the lobsters and let them cook for 3 minutes on each side. Add the white wine and continue cooking until the wine has evaporated, then add the peeled tomatoes and cook, uncovered, for a further 4 minutes.

Remove the lobsters from the casserole and place them on a warm dish. Keep them warm. Meanwhile, add the fish stock to all the juices in the casserole and crumble in the chilli and cook for a further 10 minutes. Put the lobsters back in the casserole and cook for an additional 3 minutes. Serve with linguine pasta.

Cook's tip: To peel tomatoes, place them whole in a bowl of boiling water. Leave for 1 minute, then remove them using a slotted spoon. The skins should then come away easily.

Pollo con Pomodori Secchi
Chicken with Sun-dried Tomatoes

When I was growing up, fresh tomatoes were available only from late spring, when the first juicy, red fruit appeared on the vines that covered my family's garden. So, in early spring, before the tomatoes were ripe, my grandmother made a sauce using sun-dried tomatoes – the tomatoes that we had left to dry and kept all winter. One of my strongest childhood memories is how one of my uncles would always arrive, as if by magic, when we had this dish for lunch ... perhaps he was telepathic, or perhaps he could just smell my grandmother's wonderful cooking.

Serves 4

4 chicken breasts

extra virgin olive oil

4 tbsp chopped sun-dried tomatoes, plus their oil

2 shallots, peeled and chopped

90ml single cream

125ml chicken stock

salt and freshly ground black pepper, to taste

parsley sprigs, to serve

Preheat the oven to 190°C/Gas 5. Rub the chicken breasts all over with olive oil and season. Place the chicken breasts on a baking tray and roast in the oven for 25 minutes, or until the chicken is cooked through. (Use a tray that can also go on the hob and that has sides deep enough to make a sauce.) Remove the breasts from the tray, set aside and keep warm.

Transfer the baking tray to the hob, add the tomatoes (with their oil) and the shallots and cook for 1 minute. Stir in the cream and stock and cook, stirring continuously, for a further 5 minutes to warm through.

Serve the chicken with the sauce poured over and garnished with parsley sprigs. I like to serve this dish with sautéed potatoes.

Petto d'Anatra al Vin Santo
Duck Breast in Vin Santo

Strong in flavour and potentially dry in texture, duck meat needs something to make it sweeter and more delicate. That's why in most restaurants you'll find it *à l'orange*. However, for my own restaurant I wanted to do something different, something Tuscan. When I thought about it, the answer was simple – duck with Vin Santo, Tuscan sweet wine. Perfect.

Serves 4

2 duck breasts

165ml extra virgin olive oil,
  plus extra for dressing the rocket

1 tbsp demerara sugar

1 tbsp honey

125ml Vin Santo or sweet sherry

salt and freshly ground black pepper,
  to taste

rocket, to serve

balsamic vinegar, to serve

Cut each duck breast into two to create two chunky pieces of duck from each breast. Heat the oil in a large frying pan, then add the duck. First seal the meat all over, then continue cooking over a high heat for 5–7 minutes, depending on the thickness of the breasts (if thin, cook for 5 minutes), but remember that the duck should be served rare in this dish. Season with salt and pepper.

Remove the duck meat from the pan and add the sugar, honey and Vin Santo to the juices that are left behind. Stir continuously until the mixture in the pan thickens to create a sauce.

Turn the heat to low, then cut the duck meat into very fine slices and use a spatula to return the duck to the pan. Baste the duck all over with the sauce, then transfer to a serving dish and pour over the remaining sauce. Serve with some rocket tossed in balsamic vinegar and olive oil.

Lumache nel Guscio
Snails in Shells

We never bought snails when I was a child. Instead, we went out into the fields early on 1 May (a feast day) and found the snails for ourselves, picking them from their homes in the dewy grass. When we got our hoard home, we put all the snails into a big casserole, cooked them, packed them up as a picnic and took them back into the countryside to eat them outdoors.

Serves 6–10

60 snails in their shells, cleaned and dried

50g butter, diced, plus extra for frying

2 bay leaves

1 sprig thyme

2 dried red chillies, crushed

1 glass sparkling white wine

6 garlic cloves, peeled and chopped

50g parsley, chopped

50g breadcrumbs

salt and freshly ground black pepper, to taste

Bring a large pan of salted water to the boil, add the snails and boil them for 10 minutes, then drain them and set aside.

Preheat the oven to 200°C/Gas 6. Melt a knob of butter in a casserole, add the bay leaves, thyme and chillies, and season with salt and pepper. Pour in the sparkling wine and cook gently, uncovered, until the wine has evaporated, then set aside.

Mix together the diced butter, garlic, parsley and breadcrumbs and some salt and pepper to make a dry yet soft mixture. Using a pin, remove the snail flesh from one of the shells, part fill it with a little of the breadcrumb mixture, put the snail flesh back into the shell and seal the opening with more breadcrumbs. Repeat for all the snails. Place the stuffed shells in an ovenproof dish and bake them in the preheated oven for 10–15 minutes. When the snails are ready, gently warm through the sauce and pour it over to serve.

Coniglio alla Contadina
Farmhouse Rabbit

In cooking terms, *alla contadina* means with rosemary and garlic – the way the Tuscan farmhands would cook their food. This heartwarming dish used to go a long way: even though a rabbit is relatively small, everyone would get a piece of meat and lots of sauce. We'd eat our meat and then take a piece of bread and dip it into the delicious sauce until we were completely full up.

Serves 4–6

1.3kg rabbit

1–2 garlic cloves, peeled and cut in half

50g butter

2 tbsp extra virgin olive oil

30g lean pancetta or bacon,
   beaten and cut into thin strips

175ml dry white wine

300g tomatoes, peeled (see p.54)
   and chopped

1 bunch of parsley, chopped

1 sprig rosemary, leaves removed
   and chopped

6 walnuts, coarsely chopped

zest of half a lemon

salt and freshly ground black pepper,
   to taste

Cut the rabbit into 8 pieces and rub the pieces all over with the cut sides of the garlic; rub generously on the protruding bones.

Heat the butter and the oil in a pan, add the pancetta and rabbit and brown on all sides. Pour in the wine and cook over a medium heat until the wine has evaporated. Add the peeled tomatoes and some salt and pepper to taste. Continue to cook, uncovered, over a low heat for a further 30 minutes.

When the meat is cooked through and tender, add the herbs, walnuts and lemon zest, stir well and add more salt if necessary. Cook for a further 5 minutes, then serve.

Insalata di Mare
Simple Seafood Salad

This dish instantly transports me to late spring. It's best made with octopus, squid, mussels and clams, although you could make it with whatever seafood is available. Your fishmonger should be willing to clean and partially prepare the squid for you; it can be very messy!

Serves 4

350g fresh squid, skinned and cleaned

juice of 1½ lemons, plus 4 lemon halves
   for serving

300ml fish stock

2 tbsp chopped parsley,
   plus extra to serve

600g fresh mussels, scrubbed

2 garlic cloves, peeled and
   finely chopped

1 tbsp chopped dill

300ml dry white wine

8 cooked Mediterranean prawns

100g cooked cockles

4 tbsp extra virgin olive oil

salt and freshly ground black pepper,
   to taste

Make sure that the 'tubes' of squid are thoroughly clean, then cut them into rings about 5mm thick. Put the rings and the tentacles into a shallow pan with a third of the lemon juice, and the fish stock, parsley and salt and pepper to taste; cover and cook gently for 10 minutes until the squid is just tender.

Meanwhile, put the mussels in a pan, discarding any that have broken shells. Add the garlic, dill, white wine and salt and pepper to taste. Cover and cook for 5 minutes, shaking the pan from time to time, until the shells open. Discard any that remain firmly shut.

Drain the rings and tentacles of the cooked squid, discarding the cooking liquid; remove the cooked mussels from the pan, using a slotted spoon and strain and reserve their cooking liquid. Shell the mussels (you can leave some in their shells, too, if you like).

Remove the heads neatly from the Mediterranean prawns, leaving the body shells and tails intact. Mix the cooked squid with the shelled mussels, prawns and cockles. Mix the olive oil with half the remaining lemon juice, 5 tbsp of the mussel cooking liquid, and salt and pepper to taste. Stir the dressing into the shellfish.

Spoon the prepared seafood salad on to four small plates. Garnish with the unshelled mussels, if you kept any back, and sprinkle with some chopped parsley. Serve with a lemon half on the side.

Variation: The salad is also delicious served on a bed of samphire, a very fine seaweed with a fresh, salty flavour, which you should be able to buy from a good fishmonger. If you can't find it, however, you could instead serve the salad on a bed of young, fresh spinach leaves.

Cook's tip: Save any remaining liquid from cooking the squid and the mussels and use it as the base for a fish soup, making it up to the desired quantity with water or dry white wine.

Insalata di Polpi e Calamari
Octopus and Squid Salad

Any cookbook that's about La Famiglia has to include this wonderful seafood salad – it's one of the restaurant's best sellers. You'll need to begin making this dish on the morning of the day you intend to eat it, as the seafood needs to rest in its cooking liquid for several hours.

Serves 6

small squid, approximately 450g
small octopus, approximately 250g
1 garlic clove, peeled and chopped
1 bunch of parsley, finely chopped
a few basil leaves
extra virgin olive oil
salt, to taste

Bring two pans of water to the boil. Cook the squid and the octopus separately (do not wash them or clean them before cooking – to ensure tender pieces of squid, I think it's better to cook them uncleaned). Cover and boil each for 10 minutes. Add a little salt, then cover again and cook for a further 5 minutes. Remove from the heat.

Leave the squid and octopus to stand in their own water for six hours. Drain, then cut the squid and octopus under running water to clean out the grit. Rinse thoroughly. Place them in a sieve and suspend the sieve in a pan of boiling water. Leave the fish to steam for 2–3 minutes.

Remove the sieve from the pan, slice and dice the octopus and the squid, place them in a bowl and add the garlic and the parsley. Mix together, and, before serving, add some fresh basil leaves and a drizzle of extra virgin olive oil.

Tonno con Cipolla e Fagioli
Tuna Fish with Onion and Beans

Tinned tuna is very popular in Italy – even the Romans are said to have had it, although admittedly in those days the 'tins' were in fact wooden boxes! It's really only very recently that fresh tuna has become so readily available. My father loved this dish and would eat it at least once or twice a week as the weather warmed up towards the end of spring – it is light and easy.

Serves 6

800g fresh cannellini beans or small
  haricot beans or 300g dried

2 red onions, peeled and finely chopped

200g tuna fish tinned in olive oil, drained
  and flaked

extra virgin olive oil

salt and freshly ground black pepper,
  to taste

If using fresh beans, boil them in a pan of water for 40 minutes. If using dried beans, soak them in a bowl of water for 30 minutes, then drain them and boil them in a pan of water for 2 hours. Drain the beans and allow them to cool.

Mix the onion and tuna together in a bowl. Add the cold beans. Season with olive oil, salt and pepper and serve.

Trota di Torrente al Mosto di Vin Cotto con Arancia
Freshwater Trout in Mulled Wine and Orange

Trout is often undervalued as a cooking ingredient and I find it hard to understand why, because fresh trout is delicious. When I was a boy, my father and I would fish together to catch the freshest trout of all – straight from the local rivers as the fish travelled upstream to spawn.

Serves 4

4 freshwater trout, approximately
   400g in total
4 tips wild mint (use garden mint
   if you can't find wild)
flour, for coating the fish
150g butter
salt and freshly ground black pepper,
   to taste
slices of lemon, to serve

For the sauce
90ml full-bodied red wine
zest of 1 orange
1 tsp honey
1 tbsp raisins
1 lime leaf, torn into small pieces
1 sprig thyme
2 cranberries

Place all the sauce ingredients in a saucepan and stir together over a low heat. Allow the sauce to reduce until you have an almost syrupy mixture, about 10–15 minutes.

Meanwhile, place some mint leaves and plenty of salt and pepper in the cavity of each fish and coat the fish with flour. Melt the butter in a large frying pan, add the fish and fry on each side until golden.

Remove any residual hot butter from the pan and incorporate into the sauce; add a fresh knob of butter in order to bind the mixture. Place each trout on a warmed plate and pour over a little sauce. Decorate with a few lemon slices, to serve.

Variation: If you wish, just before serving, you can sprinkle the fish with a generous amount of toasted flaked almonds to give a nutty crunchiness to the dish.

Branzino in Umido con Ceci e Molluschi
Stewed Sea Bass with Chickpeas and Shellfish

When I lived in Italy, sea bass wasn't as expensive as it is today, because it wasn't a popular fish in the restaurants. In spring, the fish would travel into the warmer Mediterranean sea and we would go to the local fish markets to buy a sea bass big enough to feed the whole family.

Serves 4

extra virgin olive oil

100g onions, chopped

1 garlic clove, chopped

500g mussels, cleaned and debearded

4 small squid, cleaned and cut into rings

2 sea bass, approximately 1.2kg, gutted, washed, and dried with kitchen paper

200g chickpeas, freshly cooked or tinned (drained)

150g shelled prawn tails

200ml vegetable stock

salt and freshly ground black pepper, to taste

finely chopped parsley, to garnish

Preheat the oven to 200°C/Gas 6. Heat some oil in a pan, add the onions and garlic and sauté until soft. Add the mussels, cover and cook until they open, then add the squid, cover and cook for a further 5 minutes. Take the mussels out of the pan, using a slotted spoon, and remove them from their shells (discard any mussels in shells that do not open).

Season the sea bass with salt and pepper and place in a casserole. Add the mussels, squid, chickpeas, prawn tails and vegetable stock (alternatively, use the stock produced by the chickpeas if they were freshly cooked), and season the mixture with salt and pepper. Cover the casserole and place it in the oven for approximately 15 minutes until the fish is cooked through.

Transfer the stew to a serving dish and sprinkle over some finely chopped parsley, to serve.

Gelato di Vaniglia
Vanilla Ice Cream

When I was eighteen years old, I served an apprenticeship for one month under Cesira, the owner of our local ice-cream parlour in Vinci, to learn how to make ice cream. I didn't get paid, but I did get to eat as much of her delicious ice cream as I wanted! This is her recipe, which I still use to make ice cream in La Famiglia today.

Serves 4

5 egg yolks
150g caster sugar
500ml whole milk
250ml whipping cream
1 vanilla pod
zest of ½ lemon

Beat the egg yolks and sugar together in a large bowl. Gently heat the milk and whipping cream together in a pan with the vanilla pod and the lemon zest. Stir to combine, then bring the mixture to the boil. Add the egg and sugar mixture to the saucepan and stir. Pour the mixture into a bain-marie (double saucepan) and cook gently until the temperature reaches 85°C on a sugar thermometer. Remove the mixture from the heat, strain into a bowl and then pour it into an ice-cream maker. Follow the manufacturer's instructions, then chill, if necessary, in the freezer until hard.

Gelato d'Arancia della Cesira
Cesira's Orange Sorbet

Cesira (see opposite) made all kinds of artisan ice creams and sorbets for us – but only during the hotter months of spring and through the summer. Back then, no one in Vinci would dream of eating ice cream in winter as we do now! This recipe is one of my favourites from her repertoire of springtime ices.

Serves 6

8 good-quality oranges
350g sugar
juice of 1 lemon
60g candied lemon, finely diced

Slice six of the oranges horizontally, just above the 'equator', and scoop out the insides with a jagged knife (take care not to cut the white pith which you need to remove later). Put the pulp in a bowl, removing the pips, and put the empty orange halves to one side. Crush the pulp with a wooden spoon, then pass it through a sieve, collecting the juice in a bowl.

Grate the peel of the remaining two oranges, avoiding the white pith, then halve them and add their juice to the bowl.

Meanwhile, boil 1 litre of water with the sugar and let it become slightly dense. When at boiling point, add the grated peel. Allow to cool, then add the orange and lemon juices. Stir in the candied lemon. Pour this mixture into an ice-cream maker (or into ice trays) and let it harden in the freezer for a few hours.

Once the sorbet is ready, use a teaspoon to remove the white pith from the six empty orange halves, then fill them with the sorbet and serve immediately.

Soufflé di Amaretto
Amaretto Almond Soufflé

When I arrived back in Italy from catering school in Switzerland this was one of the first dishes I made for my family – I wanted to show off what I had learned. My father was not overly impressed: 'It's very good, Alvaro, but this is food for a hotel; it's not food for serving at home!'

Serves 4

For the base
4 macaroons
5 tbsp Amaretto di Saronno liqueur

For the almond purée
75g flaked almonds
150ml whole milk
2 tbsp sugar

For the soufflé
150ml whole milk
seeds of 1 vanilla pod
15g butter
30g plain white flour
4 eggs, separated
30g caster sugar
icing sugar, sifted, to serve

Preheat the oven to 220°C/Gas 7. Grease and flour four individual soufflé dishes, 7.5cm in diameter. Soak the macaroons in half of the Amaretto (just long enough for them to absorb the liquid) and put one macaroon, cut into quarters, in each soufflé dish.

To make the almond purée, put the almonds, milk and sugar into a saucepan and bring to the boil. Reduce the heat and simmer gently for several minutes. Let it cool slightly and then blend in a food processor until thoroughly mixed.

To make the soufflé, put 100ml of the milk in a heavy-based saucepan with the vanilla seeds and the butter and bring to the boil. Remove from the heat and stir in the remaining milk with the flour and one egg yolk. Heat again gently, stirring continuously, until the mixture thickens. Whisk briefly. Add the remaining egg yolks, combine, and cook for 2 minutes over a low heat. Remove from the heat and set aside.

Beat the egg whites until stiff and whisk in the caster sugar. Blend the soufflé mixture with the almond purée and the remaining Amaretto. Carefully fold in the beaten egg whites.

Spoon the mixture into the individual soufflé dishes and cook in the preheated oven for 10–12 minutes. Serve hot or cold, dusted with a little icing sugar.

Gusci di Cioccolato con Crema Gianduia
Chocolate Shells with Praline Cream

Pistoia, our nearest town, was home to the local cinema and the most wonderful *pasticceria* (pastry shop). My friends and I would go to the cinema, clutching the two lire we needed to get the best seats in the house, but we usually settled on the one-lira seats at the back, saving the other lira to spend in the *pasticceria* afterwards – on chocolate shells with praline cream.

Serves 6

150g chocolate praline, chopped
50g caster sugar
120g hazelnuts, finely chopped
400ml single cream
6 chocolate shells
a small pot of chestnut purée
  (about 250g)
125ml whole milk
cocoa powder, for dusting
crunchy wafers, to serve

Place the chocolate praline in the top of a bain-marie (double saucepan), or in a bowl set over a pan of simmering water, and allow it to melt, then remove the chocolate from the heat. Add a spoon of sugar, 100g of hazelnuts and 300ml of cream. Stir well and refrigerate for at least 2 hours (you can leave the mixture uncovered).

Once the mixture is completely chilled, remove it from the fridge and whip it until it acquires the consistency of a mousse. Fill the chocolate shells with the mousse and place them in the fridge.

Just before serving, whip the remaining cream. Soften the chestnut purée with a dash of milk and pour it into six individual dishes. Place a filled chocolate shell in the centre of each dish and garnish with a dab of whipped cream, a sprinkling of the remaining hazelnuts and a dusting of cocoa powder. Serve with wafers.

Panna Cotta con Purée di Castagne
Panna Cotta with Chestnut Mousse

My aunt, Zia Marina, was fantastic at making this dessert. She knew that I loved it and would send a hand-delivered message (we had no phones at home then) to let me know that she'd made some and that I should run up to her house, three or four kilometres away, to claim my share.

Serves 6

For the panna cotta
20 chestnuts, boiled for 45 minutes,
  then drained
150ml Maraschino liqueur
400ml double cream
100g caster sugar
6g gelatine sheets
125ml whole milk

For the mousse (optional)
100g boiled chestnuts, blended
  to form a paste
125ml whole milk
150g caster sugar
300ml double cream, whipped until stiff

To make the panna cotta, crumble the boiled chestnuts into a bowl, pour over the Maraschino and leave to marinate for an hour. Then, spoon out the chestnuts and put them into the base of six ramekins. Save the marinade for use in the mousse.

Gently warm the cream in a small pan with the sugar (do not allow to boil). Place the gelatine sheets in a cup of cold water and leave for 3–4 minutes to soften. Warm the milk in another small pan and add the softened, drained gelatine sheets. Pour the warmed milk mixture over the warm cream and continue gently heating the mixture until it thickens slightly and will coat the back of a spoon, then pour it into the ramekins. Place the ramekins in the fridge for a minimum of 4 hours or until the cream is solid.

To make the mousse, put the chestnut paste in a bowl, pour over the milk, stir, add the sugar, a dash of Maraschino (from the reserved marinade) and the whipped cream. Stir to combine.

Serve the panna cotta either turned out on a plate or in its ramekin. If you're using the chestnut mousse, use a sac-à-poche (filling pouch) to pipe some on top of the panna cotta, or serve with a spoonful of the mousse on the side.

Variation: If you prefer, use the same quantities to make one large panna cotta in a single bowl and spoon out individual portions.

Estate
Summer

Tuscany in summer is nothing short of Italy's earthly paradise! The verdant greens of spring give way to golden tones; and the days start early, as soon as the sun rises over the hills – by lunchtime it's far too hot for working! This is when the Italian siesta comes into its own. Long, delicious lunches beneath the shade of an umbrella of fig trees, followed by gentle snoozing, are just about my idea of heaven. This is exactly how I remember the summer days in Vinci as I was growing up. We would try anything to keep cool – even the village pond, where we used to swim.

The summer evenings are long and languid. In August, when traditionally the whole of Italy goes on holiday, local piazzas all over the country play host to *sagre*, tasting festivals at which the locals come together to make mountains of pasta with a particular sauce, or to roast a particular meat *alla griglia*. Everyone eats together on long tables – families, friends and neighbours. Afterwards, the tables are cleared and there is dancing late into the night. These are wonderful occasions when members of every generation join in the festivities. Even now, if ever I am in Tuscany in August, I love to watch *nonni* dance with their grandchildren and aunts and uncles with their young nephews and nieces.

In the vegetable garden as I was growing up, summer was the time that the *zucchini* (courgettes) would ripen and we would have platefuls of courgette flower fritters as snacks, in just the same way that we might eat crisps now – but much more delicious. The courgettes themselves would find their way into sauces or be sliced into ribbons and tossed in lemon juice and a little olive oil as an accompaniment to our *secondi piatti*. When courgettes are small, shiny and ripe, they have a wonderful flavour that's lost as they get too big.

However, Tuscany's most abundant offerings for summer are fruit. The trees all over the region literally drip with juicy and delicious figs, cherries and apricots. Watermelons (which we call *cocomeri*) are as big as two footballs side by side, and have bright red flesh that drips with sweet juice. And, of course, there are tomatoes. In Tuscany, in summer, a tomato tastes like a tomato – sweet, juicy and like pure nectar.

The recipes in this chapter aim to capture the spirit of those hot, sunny days. There are salads and light fish dishes to take the heat out of eating, pasta courses with delicate sauces, and desserts that will help to cool you down. This is the way my family would eat under the shade of the fig trees – they are recipes straight from my Tuscan paradise.

Panzanella
Bread Salad

When I was growing up, we made bread once a week. A few days in, what we had left was hard and tough to eat. But we wasted nothing, so as the bread got too dry to eat in slices, we cut it into little squares and soaked it in a tomato dressing to make this popular Tuscan dish. Even today, *panzanella* reminds me of hot days, eating lunch in the shade on the *terrazza*.

Serves 4

5 ripe tomatoes
5 slices day-old ciabatta bread, cubed
½ cucumber, peeled and sliced
5 spring onions, trimmed and sliced
1 bunch of basil leaves
1 tbsp red wine vinegar
3 tbsp extra virgin olive oil
salt and freshly ground black pepper,
  to taste

Deseed the tomatoes and place the seeds in a bowl. Place the cubed bread in the same bowl as the tomato seeds and mix, so that the bread soaks up the seeds. If there is not sufficient juice in the seeds to soak through the bread, add a little water.

Chop the deseeded tomatoes and place in a bowl. Add the cucumber, spring onions and basil. Squeeze the soaked ciabatta bread to get rid of any excess liquid and place the bread in the bowl with the other ingredients. Add the wine vinegar and the oil and season with salt and pepper to taste. Toss the salad and serve.

Fiori di Zucca Ripieni
Stuffed Courgette Flowers

In Tuscany, we eat courgette flowers if they're fried (see p.82), but one day I visited friends in Rome and they gave me *ripieni*, stuffed courgette flowers – which I'd never seen before in my life! I was hugely impressed and I now often put them on the summer menu at La Famiglia.

Serves 8

20 large fresh courgette flowers, halved

200g lean raw beef mince (you can also use boiled or stewed meat, minced)

extra virgin olive oil, for frying

100g béchamel sauce (see p.197)

2 eggs, beaten

50g flatleaf parsley, chopped

salt and freshly ground black pepper, to taste

batter (see p.82)

Carefully remove the pistils and the small, green, external leaves of the courgette flowers and then wash the flowers thoroughly.

If you're using raw mince, sauté it in a frying pan for 10 minutes in a tablespoon of oil over a fierce heat, then allow it to cool. Prepare the stuffing by mixing the béchamel sauce into the meat. Bind the mixture with the beaten eggs, add the chopped parsley and season with salt and black pepper.

Open up the flowers with your fingers and fill them very carefully with the stuffing (about a tablespoon for each flower). Once you have prepared all the flowers, place a shallow depth of oil in a frying pan and heat it to boiling point. Roll the flowers in the batter, then fry them until golden and serve immediately.

Variation: A tasty alternative to the meat filling is mozzarella cheese and anchovy. Cut up the mozzarella, add boned, mashed anchovy, 2 tablespoons of béchamel sauce and a handful of stale bread chunks that have been well soaked in milk and then squeezed thoroughly. Bind it all with a beaten egg, stuff the flowers and then fry them in the usual way.

Fiori di Zucca Fritti
Courgette Flower Fritters

The absolute freshness of the miniature courgette flowers is the key to making this a great dish. My aunt Zia Rita would pick them directly from her garden for us to enjoy only in the summer months, when they were in season. Once cooked, they would arrive hot and sizzling on an enormous dish put in the middle of the table, for us to nibble on while we waited for our pasta.

Serves 6

2 eggs
150g plain flour
12 fresh courgette flowers
extra virgin olive oil, for deep frying
salt, to taste

Prepare the batter by lightly beating the eggs with a pinch of salt, add the flour and whisk to remove all lumps. Now add enough water to make a homogenous, fairly liquid mixture, about the consistency of double cream. Set the batter aside to rest for about 30 minutes.

While the batter is resting, carefully remove the pistils and the small, green, external leaves of the courgette flowers and wash them thoroughly. Halve the flowers, or cut them into three if they are large. Once the batter is ready, dip the courgette flowers into it, taking care to hold the flowers upside down for a moment to let the surplus drain off.

Heat a deep pan of oil to boiling point. Deep fry the flowers, using two forks to carefully turn them over as they cook. It is essential to serve them immediately, sprinkled with salt, while they are still crisp and piping hot.

Pomodori Ripieni
Rice-stuffed Tomatoes

This dish is my sister's speciality. Even now, when I go back to Tuscany to visit her during the summer months, I insist she makes her beautiful *pomodori ripieni* for me – and she always does, because she is so pleased to have her brother home!

Serves 4

4 large, fairly ripe tomatoes
200g Arborio rice
100g mozzarella cheese
1 stem of basil, leaves picked
  and chopped
1 egg, lightly beaten
grated Parmesan cheese, for sprinkling
100g butter, plus extra for greasing
extra virgin olive oil, for drizzling
salt and freshly ground black pepper,
  to taste

Preheat the oven to 180°C/Gas 4. Slice off the the tops of the tomatoes horizontally, just above the 'equator', reserving the tops. Carefully scoop out the insides, seeds and all. From the cut tops, slice off the very tops and reserve to use as lids, then cut up the rest into small chunks and set aside.

Boil the rice in a pan of salted water and drain off nearly all the liquid (leaving about 2 tablespoons in the pan) while the rice grains are still firm and *al dente*. Set aside and leave to cool. Once it is cool, add the mozzarella, crumbling it with your fingers, the basil and the beaten egg and season with salt and pepper. Also add the chopped tomato pieces and mix thoroughly. Carefully fill the tomato shells with this mixture. Sprinkle liberally with grated Parmesan, then place the reserved tomato lids on top.

Grease an ovenproof dish with a little oil or butter, arrange the tomatoes in it, then drizzle a thin stream of oil over each one, and place a knob of butter on top. Bake the stuffed tomatoes in the oven for about 20 minutes. They are delicious eaten either hot or cold.

Involtini di Melanzane alla Menta
Aubergine Rolls with Mint

I didn't readily eat vegetables when I was a child and my wonderful aunt Zia Tuilia liked
to indulge my preferences to make sure that I got a good variety of food inside me. She
used to make this dish so that I would eat aubergines – their flavour, which I was never
very keen on, is lifted by the fresh-tasting, summery mint.

Serves 4

100g Parma ham, cut into strips
100g mozzarella, crumbled
1 mint sprig, chopped, plus a few
   whole leaves to garnish
1 large aubergine, cut into thin rounds
1 glass white wine
extra virgin olive oil
salt, to taste

Preheat the oven to 200°C/Gas 6. Mix together the ham, mozzarella
and mint, adding a pinch of salt. Spread some mixture on top of
each aubergine slice, then roll the slices up and spear them with
a cocktail stick to hold the rolls in place. Place the rolls in an oiled
ovenproof dish, drizzle over the wine and a little oil and bake them
for 10 minutes. Garnish with a few whole mint leaves and serve.

Crespelle Fiorentine
Florentine Savoury Crêpes

Made with pancakes rather than cannelloni (tubes of pasta), this dish would appear on our lunch table on Sundays, made lovingly by my wonderful grandmother Nonna Marianna. Light, fresh ricotta cheese makes this a perfect summer dish – full of creamy flavour, but not too heavy.

Serves 4–6

For the crêpes

60g white superfine flour

2 eggs

20g butter, melted, plus extra for frying and greasing

125ml whole milk

salt, to taste

béchamel sauce (see p.197)

tomato passata (see p.96), optional

For the filling

200g spinach

200g very fresh, good-quality ricotta or cottage cheese

1 handful of grated Parmesan cheese

1 egg

a grating of nutmeg

To prepare the crêpe batter, put the flour in a bowl, tip in the eggs and salt and incorporate into the flour. Then, add the melted butter and the milk. Leave the mixture to rest for at least 30 minutes.

To make the filling, put the spinach in a dry pan over a medium heat, stirring continuously until cooked. Squeeze out all the water from the cooked spinach and place the leaves in a bowl with the ricotta, Parmesan, egg and a grating of nutmeg. Stir well to combine all the ingredients into a homogenous mixture.

Preheat the oven to 180°C/Gas 4. To cook the crêpes, melt a little butter in an omelette pan, pour in about 2 tablespoons of batter and cook gently on one side, then flip over and cook the other side – the crêpes will look like thin omelettes. When you have cooked all the crêpes, spread a little of the filling mixture over each one and roll them up like mini Swiss Rolls.

Grease an ovenproof dish (approximately 20 x 28cm), cover the base with the crêpes and pour over the béchamel sauce. Scatter over plenty of Parmesan cheese. If you wish, dot with a few spoonfuls of tomato sauce. Bake for 20 minutes.

Agnolotti al Sugo d'Arrosto
Filled Pasta with Meat Sauce

My aunt Zia Rita first made this dish for me. As I watched her, I asked her what sauce she was going to serve with the *agnolotti*, imagining that she would use a simple dressing of olive oil, sage and butter. '*Sugo di carne* [meat sauce],' she replied and I immediately thought this sounded too heavy for a filled pasta. But I was wrong – it wasn't Bolognese-like, as I'd expected, it was the delicious gravy of the roast veal that she was cooking in the oven, and it was fantastic!

Serves 6

1 quantity of fresh pasta (see p.22)
tender leaves of 1 small cabbage
leaves of 1 endive
extra virgin olive oil, for frying
2 celery sticks, chopped
2 carrots, peeled and chopped
1 onion, peeled and chopped
1 garlic clove, peeled and chopped
2 rosemary stems, leaves picked
3 sage leaves, chopped
3 bay leaves
150g veal fillet, cubed
100g pork fillet, cubed
50g ham, chopped
50g lard
185ml beef stock
2 glasses red wine
2 tbsp plain flour
50g rice (dried weight), cooked in milk
7 eggs, beaten
200g Parmesan cheese, grated
a grating of nutmeg
salt and freshly ground black pepper,
  to taste

Preheat the oven to 180°C/Gas 4. To make the meat sauce, cook the cabbage and endive in a pan of boiling salted water until tender. Drain, chop and set aside. Heat some oil in a casserole and gently brown the celery, carrots, onion, garlic and herbs. Add the meats, ham and lard and cook over a high heat for 10–15 minutes, stirring regularly. Add half the beef stock and the wine, stir, then transfer the casserole, uncovered, to the oven for 30 minutes.

Once cooked, allow the mixture to cool a little, remove it from the casserole (keeping the cooking juices in the casserole), then mince it. Sprinkle some flour in the casserole, add the remaining beef stock, place the casserole back in the oven and cook for a further 30 minutes. Remove from the oven, season with salt and pepper and then strain. This is your meat sauce.

Tip the minced meat into a bowl and add the chopped vegetables, cooked rice, eggs and Parmesan. Mix together well, then season with salt, pepper and a little grated nutmeg.

To make the *agnolotti*, roll out the pasta dough and, using a circular cutter, such as a pastry cutter, cut circles in the dough and fill each with the stuffing, using a sac-à-poche (filling pouch). Fold the pasta circles over, pressing down the edges to make the *agnolotti*.

Cook the *agnolotti* in plenty of salted boiling water for 3–4 minutes. Once they are ready, sauté them in a casserole with the meat sauce, then serve immediately.

Spaghetti Integrali con Finocchio e Acciughe Fresche
Wholemeal Spaghetti with Fennel and Fresh Anchovies

My cousin Adriana used to make this dish – including hand-making the *integrali* (wholemeal) spaghetti, using wholemeal flour from wheat that had been grown in her mother's own fields. As a result, it always reminds me of how, in my family, the most wonderful food came from the land around us. Wholemeal pasta takes a long time to cook, so you'll need a little patience – but it's wonderfully good for you and gives a great flavour.

Serves 4

200g fresh anchovies
2 tbsp extra virgin olive oil
250g young fennel, finely sliced,
  feathery leaves removed and reserved
1 onion, peeled and finely sliced
320g wholemeal spaghetti
salt and white pepper, to taste

Clean, gut and fillet the anchovies; wash them under plenty of running water and pat dry with kitchen paper or with a clean tea towel, taking care not to break them.

Heat the oil in a medium-sized saucepan, add the sliced fennel and onion and cook over a medium heat until soft, stirring occasionally. Do not allow the fennel or onion to brown.

Add the anchovies to the pan and cook for about 1 minute (if overcooked they will crumble). Remove from the heat and season with salt and pepper.

Cook the spaghetti in a pan of slightly salted boiling water, then drain. Place it in a large bowl and season with the anchovy sauce. Decorate with some of the reserved fennel leaves.

Tagliatelle con Pomodoro Crudo
Tagliatelle with Fresh Tomatoes

I can't count the times I returned home from school and called out 'Mamma! What are we going to eat today?' and my mother would reply '*Minestra rizza-ti*', which translated literally means 'Eat-and-get-up soup'! Not actually a soup at all, this is a fast, easy pasta sauce that was perfect to fill up hungry stomachs at the end of a busy day.

Serves 4

450g ripe plum tomatoes,
  peeled (see p.54), deseeded and diced
1 red onion, peeled and diced
2 garlic cloves, peeled and diced
6 tbsp torn basil
4 tbsp extra virgin olive oil, plus extra
  for drizzling
400g fresh tagliatelle
freshly ground black pepper, to taste

Mix the diced tomato flesh with the red onion and the garlic. Add the basil and the oil and stir.

Cook the tagliatelle in a pan of boiling salted water until *al dente*, then drain and tip into the sauce. Toss the pasta lightly in the sauce. Drizzle with some olive oil and season with pepper.

Risi e Bisi alla Veneziana
Venetian Rice and Peas

I have a wonderful friend from Venice, who first made me this dish when I visited her at her home. I was so impressed! Later, when we both moved to London, we each rented a room in the same lodgings, where we were treated as brother and sister by the couple that owned the house – that's how she became 'my sister of Venice', an extra member of my beloved family.

Serves 4

50g unsalted butter

3 tbsp extra virgin olive oil

½ mild sweet onion, peeled and very finely chopped

50g pancetta

25g parsley, chopped

1kg sweet, tender, fresh young peas, shelled and rinsed in cold water; or frozen petit pois, thawed

1.5 litres beef, veal or chicken stock, kept simmering

300g risotto rice (preferably Vialone Nano Gigante)

50g Parmesan cheese, grated, plus extra for serving

salt and freshly ground black pepper, to taste

Heat the butter and oil in a heavy-based saucepan, add the onion and pancetta and fry for about 10 minutes. Stir in the parsley and fry gently for a further 4 minutes.

Add the peas and stir thoroughly. Add enough hot stock to barely cover the ingredients, then cook very gently until the peas are almost tender (about 15 minutes for fresh or 5 minutes for frozen peas). Add the rice, stir and add a little more stock. Season and stir, waiting patiently for the grains to absorb the stock before you add more.

After about 20 minutes, when the rice is tender and all the stock has been absorbed, remove the risotto from the heat, stir in the cheese and leave to rest for 3 minutes before placing on a warmed platter to serve. Offer more freshly grated Parmesan at the table.

Risotto di Fragole
Strawberry Risotto

My cousin Juliano has a restaurant in Tuscany and it was he who taught me how to make this delicious risotto. Initially, I couldn't believe that it was possible to put sweet, summertime strawberries in a savoury risotto and for the flavours to work — but they do! Perfectly!

Serves 6

500g strawberries, hulled

50g unsalted butter

1 small onion or 2 shallots,
  peeled and finely chopped

500g risotto rice

2 large glasses of red wine

1.5 litres chicken stock, kept simmering

5 tbsp double cream

6 tbsp grated Parmesan cheese,
  plus extra for serving

salt and freshly ground black pepper,
  to taste

Thinly slice half the strawberries. Heat the butter in a large frying pan and gently fry the onion or shallots until soft and translucent. Add the rice and stir. Stir the sliced strawberries into the rice, then add one glass of wine. Allow the strawberries to become pulpy and let the wine evaporate. Then add the second glass of wine and stir.

When the wine has been absorbed by the rice, begin to add the hot stock, one ladle at a time. Stir each ladleful of liquid into the rice, allow the rice to absorb it and then add more liquid. Don't rush the process. After about 15 minutes, stir in most of the remaining strawberries and let them become soft and pulpy. Stir in the cream, Parmesan and a little salt. Add plenty of pepper and cook until the rice is tender, but still with a little bite.

Arrange the risotto on a warmed platter, decorate with the remaining strawberries and serve at once with extra Parmesan.

Passata di Pomodoro
Tomato Passata

No one can make a tomato sauce like my wife Letizia (see p.51 for her *pomarola*)! She is the master of tomato sauces and has taught me everything I know about them. This one is fresh and light, and uses the first ripe tomatoes of the summer season.

Serves 6

2kg fresh tomatoes (ripe but not
   overripe), chopped into four pieces
2 onions, peeled and sliced
4 garlic cloves, peeled and crushed
80ml extra virgin olive oil
basil leaves, to garnish

Place the tomatoes in a large saucepan. Add the onions and garlic, bring up to the boil and cook for 15 minutes. If the tomatoes are too watery, let them cook for an additional 10 minutes.

Pass the tomatoes through a strainer to remove all the seeds and skins and give a smooth sauce. Pour the sauce into a bowl and stir in the olive oil. Garnish with the basil leaves. This sauce is perfect served over any kind of pasta.

Salsa Estate
Summer Green Sauce

This sauce is excellent on top of any kind of pasta, or if you prefer try it served with grilled meat or boiled vegetables, particularly potatoes. It is eaten cold, so when I was young it was just the thing for cooling us down during the hot summer months in Vinci.

Serves 4

1 bunch each of catmint, parsley,
  mint and basil (leaves only)
2 eggs, hard boiled and shelled
100g butter, softened
juice of ½ lemon
salt and freshly ground black pepper,
  to taste

Combine the herbs and eggs in an electric blender, binding with the butter and a few drops of lemon juice. Season with salt and pepper, taking care not to overpower the delicate aromas of the herbs.

Carabaccia
Onion Soup

'Soup' is a slightly misleading term for this famous Florentine dish. The consistency is more like a light vegetable stew or broth. The bread is placed at the bottom of the bowl, so that it soaks up the delicious gravy. You can eat it hot or well chilled.

Serves 4–6

6 tbsp extra virgin olive oil

1 celery head, finely chopped

1 carrot, peeled and finely chopped

1kg onions, peeled and finely chopped

600ml chicken stock

125ml white wine

150g peas and other chopped garden vegetables, such as carrots and green beans

1 slice of white bread per person

salt and freshly ground black pepper, to taste

grated Parmesan cheese, to serve

Heat the oil in a large casserole (preferably an earthenware one, as it will distribute the heat more evenly), add the celery, carrot and onion and gently sauté until the vegetables are soft. Add the stock and the wine and cook for about 40 minutes to release the liquid from the vegetables. Then, toss the peas (or other vegetables) into the casserole and continue cooking until they are tender. Season the soup with salt and pepper.

Toast the bread on both sides, dunk it briefly in boiling water, then lay one slice on the bottom of each soup bowl. Pour over the soup, finishing off with a generous dusting of Parmesan cheese, which will melt into the broth.

Rotolo di Verdure con Pancetta
Vegetable Rolls with Pancetta

I love this dish because it epitomizes the principle of eating from what's around you, even if food is scarce. I think of it as a dish my mother served when times were hard, when we made the most wonderful food out of everything the countryside had to offer us – including delicious truffles! It looks like a salami and was sliced and served in the same way.

Serves 8

500g potatoes, unpeeled

8 large leaves of spring cabbage

200g uncooked spinach, boiled, strained and chopped

100g black truffle, grated

2 tbsp grated Parmesan cheese

200g sliced pancetta

salt and freshly ground black pepper, to taste

Place the unpeeled potatoes in a pan of cold water, bring to the boil and cook until soft. Preheat the oven to 200°F/Gas 6.

Dip the cabbage leaves in a bowl of hot water for about 1 minute, strain and place on a linen cloth, each leaf overlapping so as to form a rectangle, then flatten the leaves with a meat tenderizer.

Peel the potatoes, put them in a bowl and mash them. Add the chopped spinach, grated truffle, Parmesan, and salt and pepper, and mix until smooth. Spread evenly over the cabbage leaves. Gently lift the linen cloth and roll the cabbage mixture tightly to obtain a compact roll. Remove the linen cloth and wrap the pancetta slices around the entire roll. Tie firmly with cook's string and place on a baking tray. Place in the oven and bake for 30 minutes.

Once cooked, remove the string, place the roll on a dish and cut a few slices along the length. Serve immediately.

Cook's tip: If you cut only part of the roll initially, then more as you need it, you'll prevent the unused part from drying out.

Arrosto di Vitello
Roast Veal

In Italy, 15 August is a special day – a day of national holiday (*ferr'agosto*) and *Santa Maria*, the feast of Saint Mary. It is also the date that marks the first time my mother served up this wonderful roast veal. We ate it hot at lunchtime and then sliced the leftovers to eat cold during a nighttime picnic as we watched the celebratory fireworks light up the sky.

Serves 6

700–800g veal noisette (topside)
large knob of butter
2 garlic cloves, peeled and chopped
90ml red wine vinegar
grated nutmeg, to taste
500ml whole milk
salt and freshly ground black pepper,
  to taste

Preheat the oven to 180°C/Gas 4. Tie the meat with cook's string so that it will remain in one piece during cooking.

Heat the butter in a flameproof casserole and sauté the garlic for a few minutes, then add the tied meat. Brown the meat on all sides, then sprinkle with the vinegar and continue cooking for a few minutes to allow the vinegar to evaporate. Sprinkle with a little grated nutmeg and pour in the milk. Cover, transfer to the oven and cook for about 45 minutes, stirring and basting the meat occasionally. Season just before the end of the cooking time.

When you're ready, lift the veal from the casserole and slice it. Pour the sauce on to a warmed platter and lay the sliced meat on top.

Filetto di Vitello in Agrodolce
Veal Medallions in Sweet-and-sour Sauce

When I was growing up, my family worked for six days a week, which meant that Sunday was a special day, when everyone rested. Meat was regarded as a special treat saved for Sundays and there was a proper sense of 'Sunday best'. This is one of the dishes that my mother would serve when everyone sat around the table together to eat.

Serves 4

25g butter
1 small onion, peeled and finely chopped
1 garlic clove, peeled and finely chopped
4 tbsp red wine vinegar
300ml chicken stock
12 large or 16 small veal medallions
1 tbsp finely chopped rosemary leaves
100g redcurrants, fresh or frozen
salt and freshly ground black pepper, to taste

Melt half the butter in a casserole, add the onion and garlic and sauté gently for 3 minutes. Add the vinegar, stock and salt and pepper to taste; continue to cook gently for a further 5 minutes.

Heat the remaining butter in a shallow frying pan; add the medallions and fry until sealed on both sides. Add the rosemary, the vinegar sauce and the redcurrants, and continue cooking for a further 4–5 minutes. Remove the medallions to individual serving plates, and pour over the sauce to serve.

Variations: Try using pork fillets cut into medallions in place of veal. Add a teaspoon of honey to the sauce to make it less sharp. You could also serve the dish garnished with a couple of leaf-shaped croûtons spread with pesto sauce.

Cook's tip: If you prefer not to do everything on the hob, seal the veal medallions on both sides as above, then transfer them to an ovenproof dish with the sauce. Cover and cook for 30 minutes in an oven preheated to 190°C/Gas 5.

Tagliata di Manzo
Sliced Fillet of Beef with Corn Salad

The authentic Tuscan version of this dish uses meat from the foreleg of the cow. However, I found it too chewy, so when I put the dish on the menu at La Famiglia, I changed it to use beef fillet. It still has all the markings of Tuscan cuisine, but is made using tender meat. It's like a light steak salad, perfect for hot summer evenings.

Serves 4

1.2kg fillet of beef, carefully trimmed

6 handfuls of corn salad (lamb's lettuce)
  or watercress

125ml extra virgin olive oil

4 tbsp balsamic vinegar

salt and freshly ground black pepper,
  to taste

Cut the beef into four equal pieces. Fry the pieces on both sides for a minute or two in a cast-iron or other heavy-based frying pan, without adding any fat. The meat must be very rare indeed. Remove from the pan and slice each fillet diagonally into 5mm slices.

Arrange the corn salad on a platter and lay the slices of meat on top. Add the oil, balsamic vinegar, salt and pepper to the hot pan. Stir this all together to make a thick, hot sauce and pour it over the salad and meat. Serve immediately.

Insalata di Manzo
Summer Beef Salad

When I was growing up we wasted nothing – especially meat. We cut up any leftover Sunday roast beef and mixed it with new ingredients to create a whole new meal, which is exactly how this dish came to be. The key is to dress it beautifully. Try lemon or finest balsamic vinegar as alternatives to the white wine vinegar, if you like – and always use the best extra virgin olive oil.

Serves 4–6

400g cold roast beef fillet

2 celery sticks, chopped

1 apple, peeled, cored and sliced

4 large spring onions, trimmed
  and finely chopped

1 garlic clove, peeled and finely chopped

125ml best-quality extra virgin olive oil

2 tbsp white wine vinegar

salt and freshly ground black pepper,
  to taste

4 tbsp finely chopped parsley, to serve

Trim any fat from the beef fillet and carve into thin slices. Place the celery, apple, spring onions, garlic, oil, vinegar, salt and pepper in a food processor and blend at a fairly high speed for a few minutes, until the ingredients combine to form a smooth, creamy sauce.

Arrange the beef slices on a serving dish and surround (or cover) them with the sauce. Chill in the refrigerator for 10–15 minutes before serving. Sprinkle with the parsley to serve.

Scampi in Salsa di Vino Bianco e Peperoncino
Whole Scampi in White Wine and Chilli

I learned to make this delicious shellfish dish in Switzerland, using finest langoustine. When I took it home to Italy, my family loved it – even my mother, who was the best fish cook I'd ever known and who was very hard to impress!

Serves 4

16 large scampi
flour, for dusting
1 tbsp extra virgin olive oil
1 dried red chilli, chopped or crumbled
1 garlic clove, peeled and finely chopped
½ glass white wine
½ glass cognac
125ml fish stock
2 parsley sprigs, chopped
salt and freshly ground black pepper,
  to taste

Carefully remove the shell from the centre part of the scampi, keeping the scampi whole and leaving the head and tail on. Cover the scampi in flour. Heat the oil in a large pan, add the scampi, chopped chilli, garlic and a little salt. Sauté for a couple of minutes until the scampi begin to turn red, then pour in the wine. Allow this to evaporate for 2 minutes, then add the cognac, fish stock and half the chopped parsley. Cook for a further 5 minutes. Sprinkle with ground pepper and the remaining chopped parsley and serve hot.

Luccio in Salsa
Pike in Sauce

It was my father's belief that the only fish that tastes like fish is pike! My father and I would go out fishing to catch pike in the local rivers and bring it home to my mother to cook. This was his favourite supper, and now that I think back, I think I agree with him – it was fantastic!

Serves 4

1 pike, weighing approximately 1kg, gutted and cleaned

1 carrot, peeled and diced

1 celery stick, chopped

1 onion, peeled and chopped

1 fennel, trimmed and chopped

peel and juice of 1 lemon

500ml extra virgin olive oil

3 unsalted anchovies, crushed

1 bunch of parsley, very finely chopped

1 garlic clove, peeled and very finely chopped

1 glass of red wine vinegar

150g capers

salt and freshly ground black pepper, to taste

Bring a large pan of salted water to the boil, add the pike, carrot, celery, onion, fennel and lemon peel, and boil for 25 minutes. Once the fish is cooked, remove from the heat and allow it to cool in the broth.

Heat the oil in a casserole, add the anchovies and stir over a gentle heat until they have melted. Add the parsley and garlic and continue stirring. Pour in the vinegar, add the capers and allow the sauce to thicken over a very low heat.

Remove the pike from the pan and remove all the bones, being careful not to break the fish into small pieces. Place it in layers on a platter, adding salt, pepper, lemon juice and sufficient sauce between the layers. Cover the dish and let it rest in a cool place for at least two days before serving.

Cook's tip: You can use the same weight of mackerel in this dish if you can't get hold of pike. Use a fish kettle, if you don't have a saucepan big enough to cook the fish whole.

Triglie al Forno con Cedro
Baked Red Mullet with Lemon

Red mullet was relatively inexpensive when I was growing up, even though now it can be really very expensive. My mother loved to cook any fish, and in summer there was nothing more perfect to eat than this fantastic dish, baked simply in the oven with lemon and herbs. *Cedro* is a special Italian variety of lemon, with a very thick rind and a distinctive taste. If you can't find it, use ordinary lemon, or even lime, instead.

Serves 3

3 medium red mullet, approximately 175g each, cleaned and gutted

finely grated zest and juice of 2 lemons, plus a few thin lemon slices, to serve

1 tsp green peppercorns, crushed or left whole

3 sprigs thyme

2 garlic cloves, peeled and finely chopped

2 tbsp extra virgin olive oil

salt, to serve

chopped parsley, to serve

Preheat the oven to 190°C/Gas 5. Lightly grease an ovenproof dish. Make two or three cuts in the thickest part of each mullet. Mix the lemon zest with the green peppercorns and add salt to taste. Press a little of this mixture and a sprig of thyme inside each mullet. Lay the mullet in the greased dish, sprinkle with lemon juice, garlic and olive oil, and cover with foil.

Bake in the pre-heated oven for 15 minutes, then remove the foil and continue baking for a further 10 minutes. Serve, garnished with a slice of lemon and a sprinkling of chopped parsley.

Variation: Use small trout, instead of red mullet, if you prefer.

Cook's tip: Lemons (and limes) will grate more easily if they are cold and if you use the coarse side of the grater.

Polpi in Padella
Octopus with Garlic Sauce

A friend of mine part-owned a restaurant in Viareggio, a small town on the Tuscan coast. Called I Amici, the restaurant served the most wonderful seafood, including this delicious octopus dish. My friend cooked at I Amici for many, many years, long after I'd moved to London to open my own restaurant. When eventually I returned to Viareggio and found the restaurant, an old lady was sitting in the corner. She recognized me and said 'I hear you're doing very well in London.' 'Yes,' I replied, 'Because I'm making your dish!'

Serves 4

small octopus, approximately 500g
  (you may like to ask your fishmonger
  to prepare it for you)
90ml extra virgin olive oil
2 garlic cloves, peeled and
  finely chopped
1 tbsp fresh parsley, chopped
salt and freshly ground black pepper,
  to taste
lemon slices, to serve

Peel off as much as possible of the octopus's outer skin and cut out the eyes, the mouth opening and the yellow sac. Wash the flesh in plenty of running water and cut it into thin ribbons.

Heat the oil in a frying pan, add the garlic and parsley and sauté for a few minutes. Add the octopus and cook for 2–3 minutes, stirring. Season with salt and pepper, cover and simmer for about 15 minutes. Serve hot, garnished with lemon slices.

Orata con Carote
Sea Bream with Carrots

This dish was created in La Famiglia, and is a favourite with my chef Quinto. He is as much a part of La Famiglia as I am! It is a light fish dish that's perfect as a summer main course and it goes beautifully with a well-chilled Pinot Grigio.

Serves 4

125g butter

350g carrots, peeled and sliced

4 spring onions, trimmed and sliced

2 sea bream, approximately 1kg, cleaned, gutted and scaled

120ml single cream

½ tsp paprika

salt and white pepper, to taste

Melt the butter in a frying pan. Add the carrots and spring onions and cook over a low to medium heat for approximately 15 minutes. Season with salt and pepper and add about 500ml water.

Season the sea bream with salt and pepper and add the fish to the pan along with the cream and paprika. Cover the saucepan and simmer for about 25 minutes. Remove the fish from the pan, place it on a serving dish and keep warm. Allow the sauce to reduce, remove it from the heat, and pour it over the fish, to serve.

Carpaccio di Tonno Arlecchino
Finely Sliced Raw Tuna Harlequin

I invented this dish because I wanted the restaurant to serve a fish carpaccio, but I was too worried about serving raw fish without a sauce – instinctively it just didn't seem right to me. My creation, tuna carpaccio served with lemon juice and a light, summery salsa, is now one of the most popular fish dishes on La Famiglia's menu.

Serves 8

175ml extra virgin olive oil,
    plus extra for the serving plates

800g fresh tuna

juice of 3 lemons

1 small red onion, peeled and
    finely diced

3 spring onions, trimmed and
    finely sliced

1 yellow pepper, finely diced

1 large tomato, skinned (see p.54),
    deseeded and finely diced

1 small bunch of chives, snipped

salt and freshly ground black pepper,
    to taste

4 lemons, halved, to serve

Dot the centre of 8 individual plates with a drop of olive oil. Slice the tuna very thinly and divide the slices equally between the plates. Sprinkle the lemon juice over the tuna and let it rest while you prepare the sauce.

Mix the onions, pepper, tomato, chives and oil together thoroughly and spoon this sauce on top of the tuna on each plate. Put one lemon half on top of each portion of tuna and serve.

Gelato al Forno
Baked Alaska

In Italy, we call this dish 'Vesuvio', after the great volcano that erupted over Pompeii during Roman times. When the dish comes to the table it is steaming hot, and I remember as a child being amazed how something so hot could be frozen inside. Note that you need to begin this dessert at least the day before you intend to serve it.

Serves 12

For the ice cream
500ml whole milk
150g caster sugar
200ml single cream
1 tbsp rum, plus an extra drizzle

For the cake and meringue
300g plain sponge cake
130g egg whites (approximately 4 eggs)
130g caster sugar
a pinch of salt

Make the ice cream first. Warm the milk in a pan with the sugar, removing it from the heat just before it reaches boiling point. Add the cream and the rum and place the mixture in an ice-cream maker. Follow the machine instructions to make the ice cream.

Slice the sponge and place a layer across the bottom of a deep, ovenproof serving dish. Sprinkle with a dash of rum and place all the ice cream on top (creating a little ice-cream mountain). Cover with the remaining slices of sponge cake. Freeze for 24 hours.

Just before serving, preheat the grill. Partially whip the egg whites, just until they hold their shape. Place the sugar in a small saucepan with 1 tbsp water and heat it up to 110°C (you'll need a sugar thermometer). Without stirring, pour it like a thread over the egg whites, then sprinkle over a pinch of salt. Continue whipping the egg whites until you have a shiny, compact meringue. Spread the meringue over the ice cream and sponge.

Place any remaining meringue in a piping bag fitted with a nozzle large enough that you can fit your thumb inside it. Pipe decorative lines on the dessert. Put the ice cream under the grill to brown it slightly and serve immediately.

Torta di Formaggio
Italian Cheesecake

Another recipe from the heart of my family, this tangy cheesecake is one that my sister has always made for us – and continues to make, even to this day. It isn't baked like some traditional American cheesecakes, so it is light with a fresh, lemony tang, which makes it a fantastic summertime dessert.

Serves 6

250g clotted cream

100g mascarpone

100g sugar

zest and juice of 1 lemon, plus extra lemon slice to decorate (optional)

2 gelatine leaves, melted in 90ml hot milk

250ml single cream, half-whipped

50g butter

250g digestive biscuits, crushed

summer fruit, to decorate

mint leaf, to decorate (optional)

Mix the clotted cream and mascarpone with the sugar, lemon zest and juice until soft and creamy. Add the gelatine–milk mixture. Fold in the semi-whipped cream.

Gently melt the butter in a pan, then remove from the heat and mix in the biscuits until completely coated in butter. Press the biscuit mix into the base of a mould, then cover with the cream and cheese mixture. Leave to set in the refrigerator for at least 1 hour.

To serve, decorate the top with summer fruit (such as kiwi and grapes) or a slice of lemon with a mint leaf.

Tartelette di Frutti di Bosco
Fruits of the Forest Tartlets

As children there was nothing more wonderful than to run into the forests around our home in the foothills of the Apennine mountains, and gather summer berries – wild strawberries, blueberries, cranberries and so on grew in abundance all around us. My mother would take our hoard and turn the forest fruits into these beautiful little tartlets.

Serves 4

100g plain flour
100g butter
50g sugar
6 eggs
juice of ½ lemon
seeds of 1 vanilla pod
50g plain chocolate, melted
250ml double cream, whipped
  until it forms stiff peaks
250g fruits of the forest
  (such as a mixture of blackberries,
  raspberries and blackcurrants)
icing sugar, for dusting

Preheat the oven to 180°C/Gas 4. Make a sweet paste by mixing together the flour, butter, sugar, eggs, lemon juice and vanilla seeds. Roll the paste out to a thickness of 3mm and cut out four circles to fit into four individual tartlet cases. Cook in the oven for 20–25 minutes or until golden. Leave to cool.

When the pastry bases have cooled down, carefully remove them from the cases and brush each base with melted chocolate. Pipe the whipped cream into the centre of each tartlet and cover with fruits of the forest. Dust the fruits with icing sugar to serve.

Cook's tip: To prevent the pastry from sticking to the tin, push some breadcrumbs through a sieve to create a fine powder. Lightly grease the tin with some butter and then dust it with the bread powder.

Torta di Pesche
Peach Tart

At our family home in Vinci, the garden teemed with peach trees. Every summer my mother would come into the house with armfuls of peaches that, no matter how hard we tried, we couldn't eat before they became overripe. So, to make sure they weren't wasted, she made jams, chutneys – and this delicious peach pudding, which was a particular favourite with my sister.

Serves 4

10 ripe peaches
1 large glass dry white wine
3 tbsp sugar
3 egg whites, chilled
1 tbsp unsalted butter, for greasing

Place the peaches in a saucepan with the wine and sugar. Poach slowly for 15 minutes, until the peaches are soft enough to sieve. Remove the pan from the heat, tip the peaches into a sieve and push through into a bowl to obtain a peach pulp.

Discard the poaching liquid and then return the pulp to the saucepan and allow it to boil gently to remove excess moisture. Once the pulp has become as thick as jam, remove it from the heat and allow it to cool. Whisk the egg whites until completely stiff, then fold them into the peach mixture.

Butter a 1-litre smooth-sided mould and pour in the egg–peach mixture. Place the mould over a pan of just-simmering water and allow the mixture to cook there for approximately 45 minutes, never allowing the water underneath to come to the boil. This will set the pudding. As soon as the pudding is well set, remove it from the heat and allow it to cool, then turn it out on to a dish and serve.

Mousse di Cioccolata
Chocolate Mousse

Another favourite from the menu at La Famiglia, no family or restaurant cookbook would
be complete without a rich chocolate mousse to set everyone's tastebuds alight. This one is like
the interior of a Sachertorte (without the melted chocolate on top). Of course, it's perfect at any
time of year, but I like to have it as my little indulgence at the end of a light, summer meal.

Serves 4

125ml whipping cream
1½ sheets of gelatine
125g dark chocolate, broken into pieces
200ml cream, half whipped
grated chocolate, to decorate

Pour the whipping cream into a saucepan and bring it to the boil,
then reduce the heat, add the gelatine and the chocolate and stir
until the chocolate has melted. Remove the saucepan from the heat
and allow the mixture to cool to room temperature. Fold the
half-whipped cream into the mixture and pour it into serving glasses.
Place the glasses in the refrigerator for 1 hour to allow the chocolate
mousse to set. Just before serving, sprinkle some grated chocolate on
the top (a mix of white, dark and milk chocolate looks attractive).

Sorbetto al Limone
Lemon Sorbet

When I was a child it felt as though the Tuscan landscape produced an abundance of lemons – mostly from the trees in the gardens of the big houses that surrounded our home. During the winter, the farmers stored their lemons in barns; but in the summer, the lemons were left in the open for us to take as we wanted. My mother used them to make this delicate, refreshing sorbet.

Serves 4

250g caster sugar
zest of 1 lemon
500ml freshly squeezed lemon juice

Place the sugar and lemon zest in a small saucepan with 150ml water. Gently heat the mixture, stirring continuously until the sugar melts, then slowly bring to the boil. Add the lemon juice, remove from the heat and place the mixture in an ice-cream maker. Follow the manufacturer's instructions to set the sorbet. Store the sorbet in the freezer until you need it.

Zuccotto al Caffè
Zuccotto with Coffee

This typical Florentine cake is found in the best *pasticcerie* (pastry shops) up and down Tuscany. The interior is an ice-cold semi-freddo, a creamy, light variation on more solidly frozen ice cream. The cake reminds me of the queues outside the ice-cream parlour on Montecatini.

Serves 12

400g sponge cake, ideally loaf-shaped
90ml coffee liqueur
1 tbsp instant coffee powder
400ml double cream
approximately 40 chocolate drops
cocoa powder, for dusting

Slice the sponge vertically to give you rectangular slices. Cut each slice diagonally into two triangles and use these to line a round, domed pudding bowl. Try to place the slices in such a way that the pointed parts of the triangles converge towards the centre of the bowl. Moisten the sponge lining with some of the coffee liqueur.

Add the instant coffee to the cream, and whip the cream until it forms peaks. Spoon some of the coffee–cream mixture into the sponge-lined bowl. Alternate layers of cream with layers of sponge cake moistened with coffee liqueur, adding some chocolate drops between each layer, too. Cover the top of the bowl with the remaining sponge cake, cover the bowl with clingfilm or greaseproof paper, then place it in the refrigerator for 6 hours.

To serve, carefully tip the *zuccotto* out on to a serving dish and dust with cocoa powder.

Autunno
Autumn

As autumn approaches and September gives way to October, the leaves of all those olive trees, which in spring glow green on the hillsides, start to turn silvery, and the fruits ripen, until they are plump and juicy, ready to be harvested.  The olive harvest was an important time for my family. On my uncle's olive farm, all the fruit was picked by hand, and the olive oil was the finest I've ever tasted. Even today, my cousin Pietro, who now runs the olive farm, has all his olives hand picked. It's his oil, the best-quality extra virgin olive oil imaginable, that I use in all my cooking, at home for my family and in the restaurant for my guests.

Of course, olives weren't the only autumn fruit on our kitchen table. Apples, pears and peaches arrived from the trees on our lands in their bucket-loads. Often, we simply couldn't eat them fast enough, which meant my *nonna* made fabulous pickles and chutneys to preserve them for eating through the winter months. In the foothills around our land, the autumnal forest gave us fresh mushrooms, sweet chestnuts and precious truffles – delicacies that today appear on only the most refined menus. It seems extraordinary that all these amazing foods were just there for us, around us, waiting for us to pick and eat them. I used to love to go out truffle-hunting with my family dog to uncover this exquisite treasure! Then, in the garden, came the beans – cannellini and borlotti formed staples in our autumn diet and were picked, eaten and also dried so that we always had something nutritious to eat once the icy winter set in.

In this chapter, recipes such as *I Baccelli con Pecorino* (Cheese and Broad Bean Salad; see p.136), *Lasagnole al Gusto di Noci* (Walnut-flavoured Lasagnole; see p.141) and *Salsa alla Olive* (Olive Sauce; see p.148) represent perfectly the fresh foods that we had at that time of year. Others, such as *Mozzarella in Carrozza* (Mozzarella 'On Wheels'; see p.134), appear here, not because these are seasonal specialities, but because these were the dishes that, for one reason or another, my family would serve up during the autumn months – perhaps to warm me through as the evenings grew chilly, or to make sure there was not wastage as the garden began to prepare itself for winter. Autumn was a time for taking stock, for enjoying the last of the fresh harvests before winter.

Torta di Ceci
Chickpea Pie

In Tuscany chickpeas were ready for picking in September or October. When the first crop came in, we always made a cake out of it – a savoury cake, flavoured with another of Tuscany's abundant ingredients, aromatic rosemary, which is everywhere! We ate the cake as a weekday snack – the kind of dish my mother would serve up quickly after school.

Serves 6

800g chickpea flour (also known
  as gram flour)
150ml extra virgin olive oil
rosemary leaves, optional
salt and freshly ground black pepper,
  to taste

Heat 3 litres of water in a large saucepan and add a large pinch of salt. As soon as the water reaches boiling point, remove the saucepan from the heat and sprinkle the chickpea flour into the water, stirring carefully with a wooden spoon, to create a porridge.

Return the saucepan to a gentle heat and keep the porridge simmering for at least 3 hours, stirring very frequently. Pass it through a sieve (it must be absolutely smooth and free from lumps). Then, add all the oil little by little and a sprinkling of rosemary leaves, if using (this will give a pleasant, appetizing aroma).

Preheat the oven to 180°C/Gas 4. Grease a shallow baking tray (approximately 30cm long) and pour in the chickpea mixture. Place it in the preheated oven to bake for 30 minutes or until the surface of the mixture has browned. Remove the tray from the oven, grind some pepper over the top and set aside. Serve the chickpea pie warm or cold, cut into slices like a cake.

Fagioli al Fiasco

Flask-cooked Beans

This famous Tuscan dish is nowadays made throughout Italy. We grew our beans on our own land – but if you had only a small garden with no space for growing beans, after the harvest you'd go to the farmer and buy your year's supply there and then. You'd store the beans in your *cantina* (cellar) where the dark, cool conditions would preserve them through the year.

Serves 4

1kg fresh cannellini or borlotti beans
90ml extra virgin olive oil
2 garlic cloves, peeled and crushed
1 small handful of sage leaves
best-quality extra virgin olive oil
salt and freshly ground black pepper,
  to taste

Shell the beans and pour them into a traditional Italian wine flask, straw covering removed (alternatively, you can use a pressure cooker). Add the oil, garlic, a few sage leaves and two ladlefuls of water. Seal the flask mouth with a towel or cotton cloth to prevent the liquid from spilling out during cooking. Place the flask upright on tepid charcoal. Leave the beans to cook like this for several hours.

If you're using a pressure cooker instead of the traditional method of a flask, cook the beans for 20 minutes. Or, if you're using a lidded flameproof casserole, cook them for 35 minutes on the hob.

Once the beans are tender (whichever method you use to cook them), pour them into a bowl, dress them with the best-quality olive oil, season with salt and pepper, and serve.

Cook's tip: If you can't find fresh borlotti or cannellini beans, use 450g of the dried versions, but cook them in a bain-marie (double saucepan) first.

Mozzarella in Carrozza
Mozzarella 'On Wheels'

This dish is by far the most popular at La Famiglia, which is wonderful for me because it's a dish that both my mother and my grandmother would make for me while I was growing up. I've no idea which of them made it first – but it doesn't matter. It's simply delicious.

Serves 4

For the tomato sauce

85ml extra virgin olive oil

4 garlic cloves, peeled and finely chopped

2 anchovy fillets

500g peeled tomatoes (the Italian tinned plum tomatoes will do)

1 dried red chilli, crushed

2 tbsp dried oregano

salt and freshly ground black pepper, to taste

For the wheels

2 125g mozzarella cheese balls, cut into 1cm slices

16 slices of white bread

flour, for dusting

1 egg, beaten

extra virgin olive oil, for deep frying

To make the tomato sauce, heat the olive oil in a frying pan. Add the garlic and anchovy fillets. Fry until the garlic begins to brown, then add the peeled tomatoes and crush with a fork to obtain a pulp. Add salt and pepper to taste and the chilli. Cook for a further 10 minutes, remove from the heat and add the oregano. Keep the sauce warm.

Place a slice or two of the mozzarella (see tip, below) between two slices of white bread, to make a sandwich. Repeat with the remaining mozzarella rounds and slices of bread until you have 8 sandwiches. Using the blunt edge of a round cutter with a diameter of 10cm, cut through the sliced bread and the mozzarella, being careful not to cut yourself on the sharp edge (use a tea towel to press down safely). This seals the edges of the bread around the mozzarella, creating a wheel. Repeat for the remaining mozzarella sandwiches. Coat each wheel with flour and beaten egg.

Heat a good quantity of oil in a deep saucepan. Add the mozzarella wheels and deep fry for 4 minutes. Drain well, place the wheels on a plate and serve with the warm tomato sauce on the side.

Cook's tip: Use the slice of mozzarella from the middle of each ball as a guide to how much cheese you need to fill each wheel. From the middle, one slice will be enough, but if the mozzarella slices have come from the ends of the balls, you may need two.

I Baccelli con Pecorino
Cheese and Broad Bean Salad

My mother used to make this when she and my father invited friends over for an afternoon drink – it made the perfect snack to accompany a glass of wine for our guests. To make it, you'll need a nice basketful of broad beans, preferably small and fresh. You can tell they are fresh if, on snapping open the pod, they 'sing' – that is, they make a sharp, cheerful sound.

Serves 6–8

2kg broad beans, shelled
extra virgin olive oil
8 slices semi-soft Pecorino cheese
  (non-matured)
salt, to taste
red chicory (radicchio), to serve
1 bunch of basil or catmint,
  leaves picked, to serve

Place the beans in a saucepan with a trickle of olive oil, a little salt and 2 tablespoons of water. Cover the pan and bring to the boil for a few minutes, until the beans are cooked. Once cooked, they will appear wrinkled but must be *al dente* or crisp to the bite. Drain the beans and leave to cool.

Arrange the cooled beans on individual serving plates. Sprinkle a little olive oil over each plate and check the salt. Pare the cheese and arrange three or four slices around the broad beans. For a touch of colour, add a few leaves of radicchio rosso on the side and sprinkle over some basil or catmint leaves.

Crostini con Fegatini di Pollo
Chicken Liver Toasts

A famous Tuscan antipasto, this is my favourite type of crostini. When I lived in Italy, it was especially delicious because the topping was made with chicken livers from the chickens on our family farm. Although we ate them at all times of year, these crostini remind me especially of the feast of the *Immacolata*, on 8 September, when we celebrated the birth of the Virgin Mary – they always appeared on the table as we waited for our pasta.

Serves 8

90ml extra virgin olive oil

1 leek, white part only, trimmed and finely chopped

2 celery sticks, finely chopped

300g chicken livers, roughly chopped and bile sac removed

200ml dry white wine

150g capers, rinsed and finely chopped

240ml chicken stock, kept simmering

salt and freshly ground black pepper, to taste

small slices of country-style bread or *frusta da crostini*, toasted, to serve

Heat most of the oil in a frying pan and sauté the leek and celery until golden. Add the chicken livers, season with salt and pepper and fry for a few minutes. Sprinkle with the white wine and stir with a wooden spoon, scraping the bottom of the pan, until the wine has evaporated, about 10 minutes.

Add the capers and cook for a further 15 minutes, stirring all the time and adding a little hot stock from time to time to keep the mixture moist. Bear in mind, however, that the dish must be quite thick, rather than runny.

Remove the pan from the heat, lift out the chicken livers and chop them finely. Return the liver to the pan, add a little more olive oil and, simmering over a very low heat, stir until you have a thick and creamy mixture. Serve very hot, spread on slices of toasted bread.

Fettunta
Garlic Toast

At home we made this dish in November, when the olive harvest began, and we dipped hunks of bread into the first pressing of the olive oil. I remember stuffing three or four pieces of bread into my pocket and rushing off to the barn where we had the olive press. There, the men who pressed the olives would have a fire going to keep warm and I'd toast my bread on it and then sit beneath the press, catching the oil as it was squeezed from the olives, as fresh as it could ever be.

Serves 4

4 slices of crusty white, Italian-style bread
2 garlic cloves, peeled and cut in half
best-quality extra virgin olive oil
salt, to taste

For an authentic taste, toast the bread over an open flame (over charcoal is of course best, but a modern gas grill will do fine), then rub the cut side of the garlic over both sides of the toast. Drench the toast in olive oil (only Tuscan, of the best quality), sprinkle over a pinch of salt and serve hot (cold *fettunta* is awful).

Variation: If you wish to enjoy *fettunta* as a more substantial first course, serve it with slices of red tomato on top, with a sprinkling of chopped basil.

Gallette di Patate al Tartufo
Potato Rolls with Truffles

The flavours of autumn are, for me, summed up in this dish, which we made to embellish the main dish on the table. As a boy, I would go with our specially trained dog into the forests around us and hunt out precious truffles. I was very lucky and always found one or two!

Serves 6

500g potatoes
125g butter
200g button mushrooms, diced
1 spring onion, trimmed and chopped
100g black truffle, diced
4 egg yolks, beaten
1/2 tsp nutmeg
2 tbsp grated Parmesan cheese
flour, for dusting
250g breadcrumbs
salt and freshly ground black pepper, to taste

Place the unpeeled potatoes in a pan of cold water, bring the water to the boil and cook the potatoes until almost done (they should remain firm). Drain, peel and mash the potato in a bowl.

Melt the butter in a saucepan, add the mushrooms and spring onion, season with salt and pepper, and sauté. When cooked, tip the mushroom and onion into the bowl of potato, along with the truffle, 3 beaten egg yolks, and the nutmeg and Parmesan, and season with salt and pepper. Mix well. Dust your work surface with flour, and tip out the potato mixture. Use your hands to shape it into a long, thinnish roll (rather like the roll you'd use to make gnocchi; see p.22), then cut it into pieces about 2.5cm long.

Dust the slices with flour, dip them in the remaining beaten egg yolk, coat with breadcrumbs and fry a few at a time in hot butter, adding more butter as needed for the remaining slices. Serve the potato rolls hot as a taster or to accompany roasts or fried dishes.

Lasagnole al Gusto di Noci
Walnut-flavoured Lasagnole

In October and November, Tuscany provides walnuts. We used to pick them, crush them and then eat them with olive oil. Here, I have adapted that simple snack for serving over pasta. Lasagnole are flat, wide strips of pasta – if you can't get hold of them, use pappardelle instead.

Serves 5–6

1 onion, peeled and chopped
2 carrots, peeled and chopped
1 garlic clove, peeled and chopped
5 tbsp extra virgin olive oil
1 bunch of thyme, chopped
300g minced veal
500ml skimmed milk
1 meat stock cube
100g butter
zest of 1 lemon
$1/4$ tsp grated nutmeg
$1/2$ tsp ground cinnamon
1 tbsp sugar
400g fresh lasagnole (Zite Grandi)
200g walnuts, chopped
salt and white pepper, to taste
grated Parmesan cheese, to serve
parsley sprigs, chopped, to serve

Put the chopped vegetables, garlic, oil and thyme in a large saucepan and cook over a low heat, gently turning and regularly scraping the bottom of the pan, for about 40 minutes or until the vegetables are *al dente* (take care not to overcook them). Add the meat and mix thoroughly, stirring well to avoid the meat sticking to the pan. Continue cooking over a moderate heat until the meat is cooked all the way through, about 20 minutes.

Meanwhile, boil the milk in a pan and let it cool down, then pour it into a blender and mix with the stock cube, butter and lemon zest. Add the nutmeg, cinnamon and sugar, stir well and then pour the mixture back into the pan and bring to a gentle simmer. Increase the heat a little and stir well, then cover with a lid and adjust the heat to keep the mixture simmering gently. Cook for at least 30 minutes, keeping an eye on it to avoid the sauce sticking to the bottom of the pan. Adjust the seasoning, adding a little more sugar if necessary to create a bitter-sweet flavour. Stir in the meat and vegetable mixture.

Cook the pasta in a pan of boiling salted water, drain, place it in a bowl and dress it with the sauce. If the dish looks too dry, add a little of the pasta cooking water to loosen it up a little. Sprinkle over the chopped walnuts and some grated Parmesan cheese and chopped parsley. Season with a little white pepper to serve.

Gnocchi di Patate al Pesto
Potato Gnocchi with Pesto Sauce

One of my aunts, originally from Genoa, moved to live with us in Tuscany and she made wonderful pesto – although I have to admit that the first time I tasted it, I wasn't so keen; to a child's palette it tastes so strong. However, as I grew up, I learned to love it. I think pesto goes beautifully with gnocchi. Contrary to instinct, a heavy pasta such as gnocchi is well matched with a heavy or deeply flavoured sauce.

Serves 4

1 quantity of gnocchi (see p.22)
100g walnuts, chopped
100g pine nuts
6 garlic cloves, peeled
150ml extra virgin olive oil
300g Parmesan cheese, grated,
  plus extra to serve
salt and freshly ground black pepper,
  to taste
a few basil leaves, to decorate

Put the walnuts, pine nuts, garlic cloves, olive oil and Parmesan in a food processor and blend to form the pesto sauce (alternatively, you could use a pestle and mortar as my aunt used to). Set aside.

Cook the gnocchi in a large pan of boiling salted water until they float to the top (a sign that they are cooked). As the gnocchi come to the surface, scoop them out using a slotted spoon and set aside.

Once all the gnocchi are cooked, fold the pesto mixture into them and serve with freshly ground black pepper and extra Parmesan to taste. Garnish with fresh basil leaves.

Risotto di Capesante
Scallop Risotto

This sophisticated dish was a special sight on our family table. We made it for weddings and other major occasions, and I always loved it! It is best served from September onwards, as in the summer scallops open and can take on grit, but in the autumn they tend to stay shut.

Serves 6

1.5kg scallops in their shells, cleaned
100g unsalted butter
4 tbsp brandy
3 shallots, peeled and finely chopped
500g risotto rice (preferably Carnaroli)
1.5 litres fish stock, kept simmering
2 tbsp finely chopped flatleaf parsley
3 tbsp double cream
salt and freshly ground black pepper, to taste

Clean the scallops and discard the shells. Remove the corals from the rest of the flesh. If the scallops are very big, cut them in half.

Heat half the butter in a frying pan and quickly fry the scallops on both sides for 2–3 minutes altogether. Pour over the brandy and light it by tipping the pan to catch the gas flame, or light it with a taper if you're using an electric or convection hob. Allow the flames to die down, then season with salt and pepper and remove the frying pan from the heat. Reserve the scallops until required.

Heat the remaining butter in a saucepan and fry the shallots gently until soft. Add the rice and mix together until the rice is crackling, hot and shiny. Pour in the first ladleful of hot stock. Stir and allow the grains to absorb the liquid, then add some more and repeat. Continue in this way for about 15 minutes or until the rice is about three-quarters cooked. Now add the cooked scallops and all their juices, the scallop corals and the parsley. Stir together and continue adding stock as before.

When the risotto is creamy and velvety, but the grains are still firm to the bite, take the saucepan off the heat. Stir in the cream, cover the pan and leave the risotto to rest for about 2 minutes, then transfer to a warmed platter and serve at once.

Risotto con Pancetta e Porri
Pancetta and Leek Risotto

Although we can now buy leeks all year round, in fact they are in season in October, November and December, making this the perfect autumnal risotto – whatever was available in the garden at the time was the food my mother used in her dishes.

Serves 6

3 tbsp extra virgin olive oil

400g leeks, trimmed and finely chopped

150g thinly sliced pancetta, chopped

400g Arborio rice

1 litre chicken or vegetable stock, kept simmering

50g unsalted butter

50g Parmesan cheese, freshly grated

salt and freshly ground black pepper, to taste

Heat the oil in a deep frying pan, add the leeks and pancetta and fry gently until the leeks are cooked through and soft. Add the rice and stir thoroughly to coat all the grains. Then begin to add the hot stock, a ladleful at a time, stirring constantly and allowing the liquid to be absorbed before adding the next ladleful.

When the risotto is creamy and velvety, but the rice grains are still firm to the bite, remove the pan from heat. Stir in the butter and Parmesan and adjust the seasoning. Cover and leave to rest for about 3 minutes. Stir again, transfer to a warm dish and serve immediately.

Risotto con Porcini
Mushroom Risotto

During October, my family and I would spend many happy hours picking porcini mushrooms from the forest around our home. There were so many! Once we'd gathered our hoard, we'd bring it home so that my mother could make it into this delicious risotto.

Serves 4

25g dried porcini mushrooms
100g unsalted butter
1/2 onion, peeled and finely chopped
1 celery stick, finely chopped
1/2 carrot, peeled and finely chopped
300g Arborio rice
300g wild mushrooms, diced into
  1cm cubes
100g Parmesan cheese, grated

Soak the dried mushrooms overnight in a bowl containing 1 litre of water. This will also make the stock required for the risotto.

Melt the butter in a casserole, add the onion, celery and carrot and fry gently until the onion is soft and translucent. Meanwhile, in a separate pan, warm the mushroom soaking liquid to a simmer. Add the rice to the casserole, stir thoroughly until the rice grains are coated and then begin to add the warmed soaking liquid, a little at a time. Stir continuously over a medium heat, adding more of the soaking liquid when the previous batch has been absorbed. The whole process will take 20–25 minutes, depending on the make of the rice you're using (the cooking time for risotto rice is usually written on the packets).

Add the fresh and soaked dried mushrooms to the risotto 10 minutes before you finish adding all the stock, and stir well. The rice should be *al dente*, which means that the grains should still be firm to the bite but not raw inside. Stir in the Parmesan 3 minutes before the end of the cooking time. Let the risotto rest for about 5 minutes before serving.

Salsa alla Olive
Olive Sauce

This delicious sauce is perfect served with short pasta, particularly pennette and rigatoni. These types of pasta combine well with it because they are shaped like small tubes, trapping the sauce inside as well as coating the outside. However, at home we didn't used to eat it with pasta at all – we would make it without the tomatoes, spread thickly over bread, like butter.

Serves 6

125ml extra virgin olive oil

4 red onions, peeled and chopped

2 garlic cloves, peeled and chopped

100g sweet black olives, pitted and halved, then puréed

100g green olives, pitted and halved, then puréed

100g garlicky green olives, pitted and halved, then puréed

50g garlicky black olives, pitted and halved, then puréed

450g puréed fresh or tinned tomatoes

2 medium dried red chillies, crushed

salt, to taste

Heat the oil in a pan, add the onions and garlic and brown gently. Add all the olives and cook gently over a medium heat for about 15 minutes, stirring with a wooden spoon, so that the olives are fully blended with the onions. Add the tomatoes and continue cooking, uncovered, over a medium heat for about 1 hour, stirring frequently. Season with lots of crushed chilli pepper and salt.

Cook's tip: Use a little of the olives' seasoning liquid to loosen the purées before cooking, if necessary.

Acquacotta
Tomato and Bread Soup

This is the poorest dish from the forest! In fact, even the name tells you of its humble origins: literally translated *acquacotta* means 'cooked water'! We ate it because sometimes, particularly during the war, onions, tomatoes and stale bread were all we had. But today it's a famous Tuscan dish that appears on the menus of the most sophisticated Italian restaurants!

Serves 5–6

extra virgin olive oil, for frying
3 red onions, peeled and chopped
1 yellow pepper, chopped
1 celery stick, chopped
3 ripe tomatoes, sieved to make a pulp
8 slices of stale white bread, toasted
3 eggs, beaten

Heat some olive oil in a frying pan, add the onion and sauté until the edges become golden, then add the pepper, celery and tomato pulp. Leave to cook slowly, uncovered, for about 1 hour, then transfer to a casserole and add about 1 litre of water. Bring to the boil and boil for 10 minutes.

Meanwhile, divide the toasted bread equally between your soup bowls, pressing it down into the bases. Fill each bowl with some soup and some of the beaten eggs. Leave to stand for a moment, then serve.

Minestra d'Uova
Egg Soup

This is my mother's own flu remedy, which she would always prepare when we caught our first colds, usually towards the end of autumn. As soon as I started to feel unwell, she would present me with a bowl of this steaming, hot soup, made with that wonderful cure-all chicken stock and a fortifying egg to help me recuperate. It's delicious and still one of the best comfort foods I know.

Serves 4

1.2 litres chicken stock
4 egg yolks, beaten
juice of 1/2 lemon
125g Parmesan cheese, grated
4 slices ciabatta bread, toasted, to serve
  (optional)

Place the chicken stock in a saucepan and bring it to the boil over a medium heat. While the stock is boiling, add the beaten egg yolks to the broth, stirring all the time. Add the lemon juice, sprinkle the Parmesan on top and serve immediately.

If you wish, place a slice of toasted ciabatta bread on top of the broth after pouring it into soup bowls.

Pasta e Fagioli
Thick Bean Soup

We serve this dish as a starter now, but actually it is a thick, filling soup that in good quantities provides a meal in itself. When I was very young, we didn't have a car and it gave us energy for all the walking we had to do!

Serves 6

450g fresh cannellini or borlotti beans
  or 225g dried
75ml extra virgin olive oil
4 garlic cloves, peeled and chopped
1 tbsp tomato purée
bouquet garni of 3 rosemary sprigs, tied
325g short pieces of fresh pasta, or any
  pasta cut into short pieces
salt and freshly ground black pepper,
  to taste

If using dried beans, soak them in cold water for 24 hours, then drain them, rinse them thoroughly and boil them quickly in a pan of fresh water for 5 minutes. Drain and reserve. If you're using fresh beans, cook them in a pan of boiling slightly salted water for about 35 minutes, then drain and reserve.

Heat the oil in a saucepan, add the garlic and fry until it is well browned, then add the beans. Stir together and cover with 1.5 litres of cold water. Cover the pan and simmer slowly for about 1½ hours, or until the beans are tender.

Stir in the tomato purée, season with salt and pepper, and add the rosemary sprigs. Simmer the soup with the lid on for about 10 minutes, then add the pasta pieces, making sure there's enough liquid for them to cook (add more water if necessary). Simmer until the pasta is ready, then remove the rosemary sprigs and serve immediately.

Zuppa di Cozze
Mussel Soup

This soup reminds me of lengthy family mealtimes that were spent talking, laughing and even arguing – rather than watching TV like so many suppers now – as the autumn nights drew in. My mother would make the soup in a huge cooking pot to feed the entire family.

Serves 4

1kg mussels, scrubbed, debearded and washed

1 handful of flatleaf parsley, chopped

90ml extra virgin olive oil

2 garlic cloves, peeled and finely chopped

200g cherry tomatoes, halved; or 200g regular tomatoes, quartered

90ml dry white wine

4 slices of stale bread, toasted

salt and freshly ground black pepper, to taste

Place the mussels in a saucepan over a medium heat with the parsley (reserve 1 tablespoon of the chopped parsley for later). Heat gently until all the mussel shells have opened. Discard any of the mussels that do not open and scoop the rest into a bowl. Strain the juices through a sieve into a second bowl.

Heat the oil in a casserole, add the garlic and the reserved parsley and sauté for a minute or two. Add the tomatoes, season with salt and pepper, and simmer, covered, for 15 minutes. Add a little hot water to prevent the sauce drying out.

Remove the mussels from their shells and stir them into the tomato sauce until well blended. Add the wine and the reserved juices. Simmer for about 10 minutes.

Meanwhile, place the toasted bread in the bottom of four serving bowls. Divide the mussel soup evenly between the bowls and serve.

Fagioli all'Uccelletto
Tuscan Bean Stew

Tuscan baked beans – delicious! Sometimes, I would eat a bowl of these and nothing else and they'd keep me going through the day and give me energy for all the walking around Vinci. There's quite a difference between these authentic baked beans and the ones in a can!

Serves 4

1kg fresh cannellini or borlotti beans
  or 450g dried

90ml extra virgin olive oil

3 garlic cloves, peeled and crushed

1 handful of fresh sage leaves

350g ripe tomatoes, peeled (see p.54),
  deseeded and puréed

salt and freshly ground black pepper,
  to taste

If using dried beans, soak them in water for 6–7 hours or overnight. Then drain, rinse and cook them in plenty of boiling water until soft, about 1–1½ hours, then drain. If using fresh beans, shell them and boil them in slightly salted water for 30–35 minutes, then drain.

Heat the oil in a pan and add the garlic, the sage leaves and a sprinkling of pepper. Fry until the garlic is golden, then add the cooked beans and the puréed tomatoes. Cook, uncovered, for 10 minutes. Check that the beans are well seasoned and adjust the salt and pepper before serving, if necessary.

Saltimbocca alla Romana
Veal Slices with Ham and Sage

Although we had our own cows on the farm and we generally didn't have to buy beef and veal from the markets, veal particularly was special and saved for Sunday gatherings. Veal can have a light flavour, so to make it really tasty we would embellish it with sage.

Serves 4

4 large sage leaves
4 veal escalopes, about 120g each
4 slices of Parma ham
flour, for dusting
50g butter
1 glass white wine

Place a sage leaf in the middle of each veal escalope and top with a slice of ham. Dust the side of the veal not covered in ham with flour.

Melt the butter in a frying pan, add the veal and cook for about 3 minutes (if you wish, use a cocktail stick to keep the ham and sage leaf in place). Add the white wine and cook for a further 10 minutes. Transfer to a serving plate and serve with roast potatoes.

Braciole Ripiene al Tartufo
Stuffed Veal Cutlets

Autumn was the season for truffle hunting in the forests around Vinci, and the whole village would set out to find these treasures. When we got home, we'd all enjoy a feast of veal cutlets with rare white truffle – but we'd eat only those that were too ugly to sell. Even then white truffle was such a find that it was better to sell it for cash if we could.

Serves 8

8 veal cutlets (cut from the best
  end of loin)
2 eggs, beaten and salted
100g white truffle
100g Emmental cheese, thinly sliced
30g dry breadcrumbs
100g butter

Flatten the meat lightly and allow to stand for a while in the salted beaten egg.

Place the truffle on a damp tea towel and clean it by rubbing it delicately, then slice very thinly. Cover the cutlets with slices of truffle and cheese. Fold the sides over, pressing down carefully, dip the cutlets in beaten egg and coat them with breadcrumbs. Remove any excess crumbs by gently shaking the cutlets.

Melt the butter in a frying pan, add the cutlets and cook for 15 minutes over a medium heat, allowing them to brown all over.

Polpetta di Cinghiale Marinato al Vino Bianco
Wild Boar Burger Marinated in White Wine

Wild boar roam freely around the Tuscan countryside – in fact, nowadays, they are so abundant that winemakers fear them because they rampage through vineyards, destroying the precious grape crops. When I was young, though, there weren't so many, and those we caught always made a great feast! These burgers are laced with black truffle, making them extra special.

Serves 4

550g wild boar loin, boned and cut
   into 5cm cubes
1½ glasses dry white wine
2 spring onions, trimmed and sliced
1 celery stick, chopped
50g fat from the loin
2 dried bay leaves, ground to a powder
80g sliced pancetta
extra virgin olive oil, for frying
1 tbsp pine nuts
½ pear, peeled, cored and diced
60g black truffle, diced
knob of butter
salt and freshly ground black pepper,
   to taste

Place the wild boar in a bowl with 1 glass of white wine, half the spring onions and the celery. Leave to marinate overnight.

Remove the meat from the marinade and blend it in a food mixer with the fat, salt, pepper and a pinch of dried bay leaf powder. Shape the meat into four burgers, wrap them in pancetta and tie them with cook's string. Heat some oil in a frying pan, add the burgers and fry for approximately 4 minutes.

Turn the burgers, keep cooking and add the remaining spring onion, the remaining wine and the pine nuts and cook for another 10 minutes. Remove the burgers from the pan and keep warm.

Allow the cooking sauce to reduce in the pan until it has the consistency of a good gravy, and add the pear, truffle, butter, a pinch of salt and some pepper, to taste. Remove the string from the burgers and add them to the sauce, turning once. Take out the burgers and serve them very hot with the sauce drizzled over.

Arrosto di Maiale
Roast Pork Loin

Pork was always the cheapest meat we could buy, apart from poultry, which meant that it regularly made an appearance on my mother's menu. In particular, everyone loved this wonderful roast pork – the whole family would sit around the table on a Sunday and enjoy it.

Serves 6

1.5kg loin of pork on the bone
  (must be on the bone, as this
  improves the flavour)
2–3 garlic cloves, peeled and chopped
1 sprig rosemary, broken up into small
  stems
extra virgin olive oil
salt and whole black peppercorns

Preheat the oven to 180°C/Gas 4. Roll the loin of pork in the garlic and a sprinkling of salt and some whole black peppercorns. Use a knife to make little slits all over the meat and press the rosemary pieces into the holes. If you wish, press some peppercorns into the slits, too. Heat a little olive oil in casserole, add the joint and seal the meat on all sides.

Transfer the casserole to the oven for two hours, until the meat is cooked through and has released a wonderful gravy. To serve, place the meat in the centre of a warmed platter surrounded by seasonal vegetables. This dish is also delicious eaten cold, carved thinly and washed down with some good red wine.

Cook's tip: While it's cooking, the meat will produce a gravy. Don't waste it! You can use it to cook potatoes, turnips, Swiss chard, cabbage or spinach to make an excellent, appetizing side dish.

Torta di Baccalá
Salt Cod Fishcake

When the evenings start to close in in late autumn, I am always reminded of my mother making meals using *baccalá* (salt cod), which she did two or three times a week – although then as now I could have eaten it every day for a month! This fishcake is one of my favourites.

Serves 6

1 fillet of *baccalá*, soaked for
  24 hours under slow-running water.
250ml extra virgin olive oil, plus extra
  for shallow frying
1 garlic clove, peeled and chopped
500g tomato pulp
knob of butter, plus extra for greasing
1 tbsp plain flour, plus extra for dusting
500ml whole milk
200g Arborio rice
a pinch of crushed, dried red chilli

Preheat the oven to 180°C/Gas 4. Cut the *baccalá* fillet into chunks, coat with flour and deep fry in oil until golden on both sides. Remove the fish from the pan with a slotted spoon and set aside.

Heat the oil in a saucepan, add the garlic and tomatoes, stir, then add the fish and cook over a medium heat for 20 minutes. Meanwhile, make a béchamel sauce with the butter, flour and milk (see p.197). Drain any excess oil from the tomato and fish sauce and then pour in the béchamel sauce. Stir to combine.

Cook the rice in a pan of boiling salted water until the grains are cooked but still firm. Drain.

Mix all the different elements together in a bowl, adding a pinch of chilli pepper. Grease and dust with flour an ovenproof dish. Pour the mixture into the prepared dish, allowing it to settle. Put the dish in the oven to bake for about 40 minutes. To serve, cut the fish cake into portions and scoop out using a fish slice.

Insalata di Tonno con Olive
Tuna and Olive Salad

Tinned tuna, of course, was one of those foods that was always available, even when others were scarce at the end of autumn and during the encroaching winter. My mother would make this tuna salad for us to make sure we got our nutrients.

Serves 6

1 yellow pepper
1 green pepper
500g tinned tuna, drained
4 eggs, hard boiled, shelled
  and cut into wedges
100g green olives, pitted
8 tomatoes, halved or quartered
10 anchovy fillets
100g black olives, pitted
150ml extra virgin olive oil
salt and freshly ground black pepper,
  to taste

Preheat the grill, then gently grill the peppers, turning them regularly, just to loosen the skin. Remove the peppers from the heat, and peel away the skin. Halve the skinned peppers, discard the seeds and cut the flesh into strips.

Place the tuna into a serving dish, decorate the top with a few of the wedges of egg and then arrange the green olives, green pepper slices, the tomatoes, the anchovy fillets and the remaining egg wedges around the tuna. Surround the design with black olives, and garnish with the yellow pepper strips. Season the oil with salt and pepper and spoon over the salad.

Spiedino di Pesce al Vin Santo
Fish Kebabs with Vin Santo

I learned to make this dish when I worked in the Excelsior Hotel in Florence when I was only seventeen years old. We would make it with whatever fish was available, and to me this is the typical late-autumn fish dish. I still make it in La Famiglia when this time of year comes round.

Serves 4

8 bay leaves

2 green or red peppers, chopped into 2.5cm squares

600g monkfish, boned and cut into 3cm cubes

600g fresh tuna, boned and cut into 3cm cubes

100g flour

200ml extra virgin olive oil

200ml dry Vin Santo

400g spinach

salt and freshly ground black pepper, to taste

2 small lemons, halved, to serve

Make up four skewers by following this sequence: a bay leaf, a piece of pepper, one type of fish, pepper, another type of fish, pepper, and so on, until the skewer is full and ending with another bay leaf. Dust the contents of each skewer well with flour.

Heat some of the olive oil in a frying pan and cook the kebabs over a high heat until they are brown on all sides, about 3 minutes on each side. Remove some of the excess oil, add the Vin Santo to the pan and cook for a further 5 minutes. Keep warm while you wilt the spinach, squeeze it a little and then toss it in olive oil.

Divide the spinach up between four serving plates. Remove the skewered fish from the pan and use a fork to push each serving of fish and peppers on to a bed of spinach. Remove the bay leaves if you prefer. Return the sauce to the heat, reduce a little and then pour it over the skewers. Add salt and pepper according to taste and serve with a lemon half.

Variation: You can use as many as four types of fish on each skewer, if you like. Salmon and medium–large prawns (peel the prawns) also work really well. The dish is also delicious served with a sprinkling of pesto sauce around the edge of the plate.

Zabaglione
Sweet Wine Custard

Although now we think of custard as an accompaniment to a dessert, in Italy *zabaglione*
is a dessert in itself. My mother would give us a non-alcoholic version of this as a breakfast –
it was her way to make sure that, as the days grew colder, she sent us to school warmed through
and with the goodness of an egg inside us!

Serves 4–6

4 egg yolks
5 tbsp caster sugar
120ml Marsala or sweet white wine

Whisk the egg yolks in a bowl and then transfer them to a bain-marie (double saucepan), or a small basin sitting over a saucepan of gently simmering water. (Make sure that the contents of the basin are not in contact with the water.) Add the sugar and the Marsala to the egg yolks and stir well.

Beat the mixture over the heat with a wire whisk or an electric mixer until the *zabaglione* is thick (forming stiff peaks), light and hot. If you're using an electric whisk, this will take 10–15 minutes. Check that the water simmers gently beneath the bowl and the pan does not boil dry. When the *zabaglione* is cooked, pour it carefully into small glasses and serve immediately.

Variation: You can also serve the *zabaglione* cold. Once the mixture starts to form stiff peaks, remove it from the heat and continue beating it until it has cooled completely. Mix the cold *zabaglione* with whole raspberries or sliced strawberries or peaches.

Torta di Prugne
Prune Tart

Nothing was wasted during my childhood. If plums were rotten, we would feed them to the pigs, and the good plums that we didn't eat were boiled with sugar to make jam, steeped in alcohol to make flavoured *grappa*, or dried into prunes to make sweet cakes during autumn and winter. This prune tart was one of my favourites and is still found everywhere in Tuscany today.

Serves 6

For the tart case
250g plain flour
150g butter
100g sugar
20g cocoa powder
2 egg yolks
zest of 1 orange
a pinch of salt

For the filling
250g dried Agen prunes
3 eggs
75g sugar
250ml double cream

To make the tart case, mix all the ingredients together in a bowl, then tip them onto the work surface and knead them into a dough. Wrap the dough in clingfilm and let it rest for 30 minutes in the fridge.

Preheat the oven to 180°C/Gas 4. Place the dough on the work surface and roll it out into a circle. Line the base of a 25cm-diameter ovenproof dish with baking parchment. Place the dough circle into the lined dish and cover it with dried (baking) beans. Bake it for 15 minutes, then remove it from the oven and discard the dried beans. Do not turn off the oven. Cover the base of the tart with the prunes. Beat the eggs with the sugar and cream, then pour the mixture over the prunes. Bake the tart in the oven for approximately 45 minutes until cooked through.

Tartelette con Pasta di Mandorle e Cacao
Chocolate and Almond Tart

I had never seen cocoa powder until the US Army came to Vinci during the Second World War. The American soldiers would come to our farm and ask for olive oil, butter, flour and all manner of things to cook with, which we always gave them readily. I was a boy of seven years old, and I loved nothing better than sneaking into the US cooking tents after the soldiers' visits and stealing whatever was around – that's when I first saw cocoa powder!

Serves 8

For the tart case
200g butter
300g plain flour
3 egg yolks
100g sugar
50g almonds, finely chopped
a pinch of salt

For the filling
150g butter, softened
150g sugar
125g almonds, chopped
3 tbsp cocoa powder, sifted
40g potato flour
2 egg yolks
icing sugar, for dusting

To make the tart case, place the butter and the flour in a bowl and use your fingers to work the mixture into a crumble. Transfer it to the worktop. Place the egg yolks in the middle of the mixture with the sugar, almonds and salt. Knead the dough quickly with your fingertips to avoid splitting, then wrap it with clingfilm and place it in the fridge for approximately 30 minutes. Meanwhile, preheat the oven to 180°C/Gas 4.

To make the tart filling, thoroughly mix 125g of the butter, 125g of the sugar, and the almonds, cocoa, potato flour and egg yolks together in a bowl. Set aside.

Using a rolling pin, flatten the dough to a thickness of about 5mm, then, with a pastry cutter, cut out circles of dough to line eight 10cm tartlet cases, trimming the edges and rolling again as necessary. Fill each tartlet with the chocolate and almond mixture and place in the preheated oven to bake for approximately 10 minutes. Allow to cool, then dust with icing sugar before serving.

Variation: The tartlets are delicious with a few autumnal berries (such as blackberries and redcurrants) scattered on top. Add the berries before you dust with icing sugar.

Barchette alle Prugne

Prune 'Boats'

These individual cakes (rather like little jam tarts) were one of my mother's autumn specialities – she gave them to us as a delicious breaktime snack for school. If we could get our hands on more, we would often come away with our lips stained black from the filling. Delicious!

Serves 6

250g fresh plums or dried Agen prunes
juice of 1 orange
500g shortcrust pastry
chopped walnuts, to decorate
candied orange peel, to decorate

Put the prunes in a bowl with the orange juice and leave to soften for 1 hour. Preheat the oven to 180°C/Gas 4.

Roll out the shortcrust pastry to a thickness of 3mm. Line twenty-four oval tartlet moulds (approximately 9 x 6cm in size) and bake in the oven for approximately 15 minutes or until golden.

Whisk the softened prunes and push them through a sieve into a bowl to obtain a creamy purée. Fill the tartlets with the purée and decorate with chopped walnuts and small slices of candied orange peel.

Cantuccini
Twice-baked Almond Biscuits

The word 'biscuits' derives from the French meaning 'twice cooked', and it's the twice cooking that turns *cantuccini* biscuits into the hard, dry sweet snacks that we know. My mother would make them using the autumn harvest of almonds, and then store them in an airtight jar, where they would keep for months. We had them as a sweet snack on their own, although now of course they are often dunked in coffee – or in the traditional sweet wine of Tuscany, Vin Santo.

Makes approximately 25 biscuits

extra virgin olive oil, for greasing
250g plain white flour, plus extra
    for dusting
150g whole sweet almonds
250g caster sugar
2 eggs
a pinch of salt

Preheat the oven to 180°C/Gas 4. Oil and flour a baking tray. On a separate tray, toast the almonds in the oven for several minutes, until lightly browned. Once toasted, remove them from the oven and, once cool enough to handle, chop them roughly.

Sift the flour into a large bowl, add the sugar and almonds and a pinch of salt. Blend in the eggs and knead the mixture until you have a soft and elastic dough. Shape the dough into several small loaves and place these on the prepared baking tray. Bake in the oven for approximately 25 minutes or until they are light golden brown.

Remove the loaves from the oven and slice each one into individual biscuits approximately 2cm thick. Place the biscuits on the baking tray and return them to the oven for approximately 10 minutes or until deep golden brown. Remove them from the oven, allow to cool and serve with coffee or traditional Vin Santo or a sweet, medium or dry dessert wine.

Variation: Although this recipe corresponds to the classic version of *cantucci* biscuits, using almonds, try experimenting with different ingredients. Interesting variations include chocolate and pistachio or chocolate and crystallized ginger, which you simply add in small chunks to the dough.

Rocciata d'Assisi
Assisi Biscuits

This is a traditional Tuscan dish, perhaps adopted from neighbouring Umbria (home to Assisi). These little biscuits today are eaten as a snack to have with coffee, but at home they were made by Tuscan mothers everywhere as a sweet snack for their children.

Serves 4–6

250g plain white flour,
  plus extra for dusting
280g caster sugar
90ml sunflower oil
2 apples, peeled, cored and sliced
50g currants
75g sultanas
100g dried figs
100g chopped walnuts
100g whole hazelnuts
100g blanched almond slivers
90ml Marsala
4 tbsp icing sugar, for dusting
a pinch of salt

Preheat the oven to 180°C/Gas 4. In a large bowl blend the flour with 1 tbsp of the sugar, 1$^{1/2}$ tbsp of the oil and a pinch of salt. Add enough water to make a smooth and pliable dough (you'll need approximately 175ml of water). Roll the dough out on a floured work surface until it is as thin as possible without tearing.

Mix the apples, currants, sultanas, figs, walnuts, hazelnuts and almonds together with the remaining caster sugar and add the Marsala. Use this mixture to fill the centre of the pastry sheet. Roll the pastry to encase the fruit and nut mixture. Carefully seal the edges, then cut slices of the filled pastry just long enough so that you can bend each one into a horseshoe shape. Seal the ends of each horseshoe as you go to make individual biscuits.

Use the remaining oil to grease a baking sheet. Lay the pastry roll on top and rub some of the oil over the surface. Bake in the preheated oven for approximately 40 minutes until crisp and golden brown. Leave to cool, then dust with icing sugar before serving.

Inverno
Winter

Winters were long where I grew up, nestled beneath the foothills of the Apennines. And, just as the summers could be blisteringly hot, so the winters were bitterly cold. Every year, from just after Christmas until at least February the following year, the whole landscape around us was covered with a blanket of snow. For longer than that, the fertile soil beneath was frozen and, as a result, fresh food was scarce. It was at this time of year that everything autumn had given us that we'd dried or otherwise preserved came into its own.

One food group that was easy to come across during winter was game. During the early part of winter, wild boar, deer, pheasant and wild pigeon were abundant in the forests and across the farmland around us. Men would go out hunting every day with guns, hoping to bring home fresh meat for the mothers and grandmothers to cook with. Nothing was wasted from these animals. We used not only the meat but the offal, too – liver, tripe and other organ meat all feature in my winter recipes.

The pasta dishes we ate during winter were heavier and more substantial than at other times of year. Gnocchi made with potato, served with a rich, warming cheese sauce or tagliatelle served up with a hearty wild boar sauce frequently arrived at family mealtimes. Soup, too, was another favourite – warming all the way through during even the deepest frosts. And we always had plenty of oranges – these were Tuscany's splash of colour across the wintry, white snow.

At Christmas aunts, cousins, grandparents and siblings would all gather to eat and enjoy each other's company over the whole day. We would settle down to a feast of pheasant, goose or duck, with potatoes, carrots and other root vegetables. How much noise there would be with everyone gathered together under one roof!

At the end of winter came the start of the year's other most important religious festival. Lent, which usually begins in February, marks the beginning of the run-up to Easter. We always gave up meat for Lent and it arrived just at the time we might get the first inkling of fresh vegetables coming through in time for spring.

The recipes of this chapter chart the hardest part of the year for those living from the land – and yet still beans, mushrooms and fruit all feature heavily. Cheese, dried salt cod (*baccalá*) and other foods that were preserved and reinvented form the heart of these delicious meals. Every time I cook them I am reminded that wonderful food can be made even during the harshest winters – these are the dishes that show me that my family were all masters in *la cucina*!

Cipolle in Agrodolce
Sweet-and-sour Onions

The season for growing onions is March through to August, which meant that, when I was a child, by winter onions were scarce. As a result, my grandmother would take the last of the year's fresh onions and preserve them in jars in this sweet-and-sour pickling juice. As a village, we would always pool our resources and, during winter, four or five families would share the onions from my grandmother's jars until the fresh ones came again in the spring.

Serves 6

1kg red onions, peeled and cut
  into segments
125ml red wine vinegar
3 tbsp extra virgin olive oil
1 tbsp sugar
salt, to taste

Blanche the onions in a bowl of boiling water for a few minutes, or place them in a pressure cooker and cook them for 25 minutes, until all the juices have run out.

Put the onions in a saucepan, add all the other ingredients, then put the saucepan over a low heat – and wait. While you're waiting, stir the mixture frequently – it will gradually change consistency and colour to become thicker and darker. You'll need to leave it cooking slowly like this for 3 hours to get the best results. Store the onions in airtight pickling jars, and serve hot or cold.

Crostini di Polenta con Salsicce
Cornmeal Slices with Sausages

In Italy, polenta, now beloved of the finest Italian restaurants the world over, was traditionally a food of the poor. Tartlets of polenta were cheap to make and good for staving off hunger at the times of year when more flavoursome food was scarce. We would fill or spread our tartlets with other things to give them more flavour and texture. In this case it's a tangy onion, tomato and sausage sauce. Delicious!

Serves 6

300g cornmeal
extra virgin olive oil, for frying
1 red onion, peeled and chopped
2 spring onions, trimmed and chopped
3 sausages (preferably Italian), crumbled
  into pieces
2 tomatoes, coarsely chopped

Place the cornmeal in a saucepan with 500ml of water. Stir the cornmeal with a wooden spoon over a low heat for about 40 minutes, until you have a thick porridge. Place the cooked cornmeal on a pastry board (or in a rectangular oven tray, which is more practical) and allow to cool.

Heat a trickle of oil in a frying pan, add the onion and spring onions and sauté until soft. Add the crumbled sausages and raise the heat to cook the mixture through, about 15 minutes. Add the tomatoes and allow to reduce to create quite a thick sauce.

Cut the cooked cornmeal into triangles, each 1cm thick, and deep fry them in oil. When they are very crisp and golden, liberally spread the sausage mixture over them and serve hot.

Insalata d'Arance alla Siciliana
Sicilian-style Orange Salad

This savoury salad is made with oranges and garlic. My wife Letizia first made it and had to coax me into trying it, as I couldn't believe what she was putting in front of me! As always, of course, she was right – the flavours work beautifully; it's delicious! It makes a great appetizer or even an accompaniment to grilled fish or meat.

Serves 6

6 oranges (blood oranges are best, if available), peeled, pith removed

4–5 tbsp extra virgin olive oil

8 walnuts, shelled and crushed using a pestle and mortar

1 garlic clove, peeled and chopped

a pinch of ground ginger

¼ onion, peeled and chopped

juice of ½ lemon

a pinch of cumin

salt and freshly ground black pepper, to taste

Thinly slice the peeled oranges, then cut the slices in half, reserving 8–10 whole slices to arrange on top of the completed salad. Place the halved slices in a large salad bowl, and dress with the oil, salt and pepper. Add the crushed walnuts, garlic, ginger, onion and lemon juice. Toss together. Leave the salad to rest in the refrigerator for about 1 hour. Before serving, place the reserved whole orange slices on top of the salad and sprinkle with cumin.

Variation: This variation – called *Insalata d'Arance del Principe Demidoff* (Prince Demidoff Orange Salad) – gives a little lemony tang and an alcoholic kick. Peel the oranges and cut them into thin slices; add a thinly sliced lemon (do not remove the peel) and a peeled, cored and diced Cox apple. Dress with lemon juice, olive oil, salt, pepper and one small glass of vodka.

Pinzimonio di Verdure all'Arancia
Crudités in Orange Sauce

This is another of my wife's favourites. A Sicilian by birth, she grew up with the winter landscape dotted with oranges hanging from the trees. This antipasto, made not only with oranges but also with seasonal vegetables, is a perfect winter appetizer.

Serves 6

3 oranges

1 bunch red chicory (radicchio),
  cut lengthways into strips

1 small celeriac, approximately 200g,
  peeled and grated into strips

1 tbsp snipped chives

60ml extra virgin olive oil

salt and freshly ground black pepper,
  to taste

Juice two of the oranges, reserving the juice in a bowl. Peel the third orange, then cut its flesh into slices. Place the red chicory in the centre of a serving dish and surround it with celeriac strips and orange slices. Add a pinch of salt to the orange juice, mix in the chives and oil and whisk to obtain a perfectly combined sauce. When you're ready to serve the dish, pour over the salad dressing and season with some freshly ground pepper.

Pan di Fegati
Savoury Bread with Liver

This dish is more like a savoury cake than a true 'bread'. My mother would make a large loaf and we would eat it over the course of a week as a snack, after school or while we were waiting for lunch. It was a great way to get the children to eat offal, ensuring there was no wastage from the food we had. It's too heavy for summer, but perfectly filling and sustaining for winter.

Serves 4

half a large loaf of stale bread,
    crust removed

125ml whole milk

600g chicken, calf's or pig's liver,
    trimmed and chopped

generous knob of butter

60ml brandy

5 eggs, beaten

a few bay leaves

salt and freshly ground black pepper,
    to taste

Preheat the oven to 180°C/Gas 4. Soak the bread in the milk, then remove it and squeeze it well.

Place the liver pieces in a casserole with the butter, season with salt and pepper, and cook gently, uncovered, over a medium heat for about 30 minutes. Pour in the brandy, allow it to evaporate, then remove the casserole from the heat.

Break up the well-squeezed bread into the beaten eggs. Put the liver through a mincer and reduce it to a homogenous paste. Carefully add the egg mixture into the liver paste.

Lay the bay leaves evenly over the base of a rectangular, ovenproof dish. Slowly pour in the mixture and cook in a bain-marie (double saucepan) in the preheated oven for about 2 hours. It will set to a pâté-like consistency.

Take the bain-marie out of the oven. Using a spatula, loosen the edges of the cake from the dish and leave the cake to cool to lukewarm (try not to let it cool completely). While it's still warm turn it out on to a serving dish. Serve in slices.

Bocconcini di Prosciutto con Scamorza

Ham and Scamorza Appetizers

This is one of my chef Quinto's dishes and has been on the menu at La Famiglia for years – delicious melting cheese wrapped inside the finest Parma ham and served hot as a savoury starter. No wonder it's so popular!

Serves 4

200g scamorza cheese or any other kind of smoked cheese

16 slices of Parma ham

Preheat the oven to 190°C/Gas 5. Cut the cheese into pieces, each about 1.5cm thick and 6cm long. Roll each piece in a thin slice of Parma ham. Place the rolls on a baking tray and bake in the oven for approximately 6 minutes until the cheese has melted. Serve immediately.

Bocconcini di Daino con Verza e Mostarda di Cremona
Venison Pieces with Savoy Cabbage and Candied Fruit

I learned to make this dish while I was in Switzerland, where the winters are hard and bitterly cold. It is a rich, warming appetizer and was popular with the public who would come to try our food at the cookery school.

Serves 4

extra virgin olive oil, for frying

500g boned venison loin, cut into
  bite-sized pieces

1 spring onion, trimmed and chopped

1 small apple, peeled, cored and sliced

small jar of *mostarda di Cremona*
  (candied fruit preserve)

150ml vegetable stock

4 large Savoy cabbage leaves

salt and freshly ground black pepper,
  to taste

Heat some olive oil in a large frying pan, add the venison pieces and spring onion and sauté over a high heat until the meat is well cooked on the outside but still pink on the inside. Season with salt and pepper and then remove the meat from the frying pan.

Put the apple and candied fruit in the frying pan and cook over a low heat. Keep the fruit moist by adding a ladle of vegetable stock and continue cooking until the mixture reaches the consistency of a chutney, about 20 minutes.

Meanwhile, boil the Savoy cabbage leaves in a saucepan of water until soft, then drain them and place them on the individual serving dishes. Pile the venison morsels and the chutney on top.

Fagioli all'Olio
Beans in Olive Oil

Beans are among the most popular vegetables in Tuscany and we Tuscans eat a lot of them – in fact, Italians from elsewhere in the country call the Tuscans *mangia fagioli*, which means 'bean eaters'! This dish makes a wonderful starter on its own, or a good accompaniment to grilled meat. It is packed with healthy energy, which kept us going during the cold winter.

Serves 4

400g dried white beans
   (cannellini or haricot)
1–2 garlic cloves, peeled and crushed
1 carrot, peeled
1 onion, peeled
2 celery sticks
1 sprig sage
5 tbsp good-quality extra virgin olive oil
salt, to taste
crostini of ciabatta, to serve (optional)

Soak the beans in water overnight, then drain them and put them in a heavy-based saucepan with 2 litres of cold water. Add the garlic, vegetables, sage and a dash of olive oil. Slowly bring to the boil, then reduce the heat to low and bring back to a gentle simmer (the beans should barely be moving in the water). Cover the saucepan and cook the beans for about 45 minutes. Remove the lid, season with salt to taste, then replace the lid and leave the beans to cook for a further 15 minutes, until tender.

Remove the carrot, onion, celery and sage from the saucepan, then drain the beans and serve them hot or cold with the rest of the olive oil drizzled over the top, and topped with the ciabatta crostini, if using.

Insalata di Verdure con Verza
Mixed Vegetable Salad with Savoy Cabbage

During winter there was no lettuce to make salad, so instead my mother made salads using Savoy cabbage. To make the winter salad more interesting, she would use the chickpeas that she had dried and stored away earlier in the year.

Serves 8

1 heart of Savoy cabbage, finely sliced

1 400g tin of chickpeas in water, drained and rinsed

1 400g tin of red or green lentils in water, drained and rinsed

250g potatoes, peeled, boiled, cooled and cut into small cubes

1 tbsp white wine vinegar

1 scant tsp mustard

100ml extra virgin olive oil

salt and freshly ground black pepper, to taste

Place the sliced cabbage on a serving dish, scatter over the chickpeas and lentils, and then the cubed potatoes.

Whisk together the vinegar, mustard, oil and a pinch of salt to make a thoroughly combined dressing. Pour the dressing all over the salad and then season generously with black pepper before serving.

Insalata di Carote e Noci
Carrot and Walnut Salad

When I was a child I loved this salad! Carrots with sultanas and walnuts – which always remind me of Christmases at home in Tuscany – give a wonderful combination of flavours and textures and a great mix of savoury and sweet.

Serves 4

450g carrots, peeled and coarsely grated
1 small onion, peeled and thinly sliced
grated zest and juice of 1 orange
juice of $1/2$ lemon
3 tbsp extra virgin olive oil
1 garlic clove, peeled
75g walnuts, roughly chopped
50g sultanas
salt and freshly ground black pepper,
  to taste
2 tbsp chopped parsley, to serve

Place the carrots in a bowl and mix with the sliced onion. Put the orange zest and juice, lemon juice, olive oil, garlic and 50g of the walnuts into a liquidizer or food processor and blend until smooth. Add salt and pepper to taste. Stir this dressing into the carrot mixture, together with the remaining walnuts and the sultanas. Tip the salad into a serving bowl and sprinkle with parsley, to serve.

Variation: Try using equal quantities of grated carrot and grated parsnip; both have a slightly sweet flavour and they blend very well together. You could also try using hazelnuts instead of walnuts.

Cook's tip: Carrots discolour very quickly once they have been peeled; if you want to prepare the grated carrot but are not going to make the salad immediately, stir some of the orange or lemon juice into it and cover it with clingfilm until you're ready.

Tagliatelle con Salsa di Cinghiale
Tagliatelle with Wild Boar Sauce

Winter was our game season, and no morsel of any catch went to waste in our house. All the little pieces of wild boar left after a roast were minced up and used to make the most delicious, rich pasta sauce. This sauce is a Tuscan tradition and a favourite with the diners at La Famiglia.

Serves 4–6

1 quantity of fresh pasta (see p.22),
 rolled out and cut into tagliatelle

2 tbsp extra virgin olive oil

1 onion, peeled and chopped

1 carrot, peeled and finely chopped

1 celery stick, chopped

1kg minced wild boar meat

1 tbsp ground fennel seeds

175ml dry red wine

1 tbsp tomato purée

150ml beef stock

1 tbsp unsalted butter

salt and freshly ground black pepper,
 to taste

grated Parmesan cheese,
 to serve (optional)

Heat the oil in an earthenware or other heavy-based flameproof casserole, add the onion, carrot and celery and sauté until the onion is golden brown. Add the wild boar meat, allow to brown and then add the ground fennel seeds and season with salt and pepper.

Pour in the wine and add the purée and 250ml of water and cook, uncovered, over a gentle heat, for $1^{1}/_{2}$ hours, adding a little stock or hot water from time to time. Then, stir the butter into the sauce.

When you're ready, boil the tagliatelle in salted water until *al dente*. Drain and serve mixed with the sauce. Sprinkle with grated Parmesan cheese, if desired.

Gnocchi di Patate ai Quattro Formaggi
Gnocchi with Four-cheese Sauce

This warming, homely gnocchi dish is one of my favourites – and it is always a hit at
La Famiglia when I put it on our winter menu (potato gnocchi is a classic winter dish).
The cheeses give a rich, flavourful sauce that was one of my grandmother's specialities.

Serves 4

1 quantity of gnocchi (see p.22)
30g butter
50g mascarpone cheese
50g gorgonzola cheese, grated
400ml double cream
30g pecorino cheese, grated
30g Parmesan cheese, grated
salt and freshly ground black pepper,
  to taste

Cook the gnocchi in salted boiling water until they float to the
surface. Scoop out the cooked gnocchi as they rise to the top
using a slotted spoon and set aside.

Melt the butter in a pan and mix in the mascarpone and
gorgonzola. Add the cream and cook for 10 minutes, stirring,
then stir in the pecorino and Parmesan.

Fold the sauce into the gnocchi. Serve on a hot plate seasoned
with some ground black pepper on the top.

Gnocchi di Spinaci al Forno
Oven-baked Spinach Gnocchi

My grandmother and my mother made this dish throughout my childhood – it was one of those pastas that would always appear on a cold, frosty Sunday before we had our meat course. The gnocchi are not made with potato, but with polenta and they are baked in the oven. I love them with spinach, as here, but you could use any green leaf you wanted.

Serves 4

For the semolina gnocchi
550g fresh spinach, or frozen if you can't find fresh
500ml whole milk
1 tbsp butter, plus extra for greasing
200g semolina flour
2 eggs, beaten
50g Parmesan cheese, grated
salt, to taste

For the béchamel sauce
40g butter, plus extra for greasing
2 tbsp plain flour
500ml whole milk
a pinch of grated nutmeg
40g Parmesan cheese, grated
salt, to taste

Preheat the oven to 220°C/Gas 7. To make the gnocchi, wash the spinach leaves, then cook them in a saucepan in just the water that remains clinging to the leaves after washing. Once the spinach has cooked, drain it, then squeeze it dry using your hands. Finely chop it by hand or in a food processor.

In a saucepan, bring the milk to the boil. Melt the butter into it, then sprinkle the semolina into the boiling milk a little at a time, stirring continuously to prevent lumps forming. Cook over a low heat for around 10 minutes. Remove the semolina mixture from the heat and, using a wooden spoon, blend in the spinach, eggs, Parmesan and a pinch of salt, stirring vigorously.

To prepare the béchamel sauce, melt the butter in a saucepan and add the flour, stirring energetically to a smooth paste. Stir in the milk and continue to cook, stirring all the time until the sauce has thickened. Season with salt and nutmeg and stir in the Parmesan.

Shape the spinach mixture into small lumps, place them in a buttered ovenproof dish and cover with the white sauce. Bake for 20–25 minutes.

Lasagne di Magro
Baked Mushroom and Vegetable Lasagne

The Italian word *magro* means 'thin', but in this context it means that there's no mince inside; instead the mushrooms give the dish a good, meaty texture. We used to eat this lasagne on Ash Wednesday, the first day of Lent, usually in February, when traditionally we would give up eating meat for the forty days running up to Easter Day.

Serves 8

1 quantity of fresh pasta dough
  (see p.22), or 500g good-quality
  dried lasagne

100ml extra virgin olive oil

1 large onion, finely sliced

2 courgettes, cut into 2cm cubes

2 carrots, cut into 2cm cubes

100g shelled peas

butter, for greasing

1 litre béchamel sauce
  (see p.197, doubled)

100g mushrooms, sliced

100g tomatoes, peeled (see p.54)
  and roughly chopped

300g Parmesan cheese, grated

150g mozzarella cheese for cooking,
  sliced

salt and freshly ground black pepper,
  to taste

Preheat the oven to 200°C/Gas 6. If you're using dried lasagne, cook the sheets in boiling water until they're *al dente* (for the best results, do this even if the packet says that no precooking is required).

If you're making your own lasagne, make the pasta in the usual way (see p.22), then taking a small piece at a time, roll it out to strips of thin dough, 1–1.5mm thick. Cut each long strip into suitable lengths to fit your lasagne dish.

Heat the olive oil in a large saucepan and add the onion. Fry until translucent and soft and then stir in the courgettes, carrots and peas. Cook for about 10 minutes, uncovered, stirring continuously, until the vegetables are cooked, but *al dente*.

Grease a deep baking dish (10 x 30 x 30cm). Pour in 250ml of the béchamel sauce. Add a layer of lasagne sheets, making sure the sheets don't overlap, and cover with a ladleful of the vegetables, followed by a ladleful of the béchamel sauce, then a small handful each of sliced mushrooms and chopped tomatoes and 2 tablespoons of Parmesan. Cover with another layer of lasagne sheets and repeat the process until all the ingredients are finished. Top with the sliced mozzarella and bake in the oven for 25 minutes. Once cooked, leave the lasagne to rest for 10 minutes before serving.

Farinata con Cavolo Nero
Polenta with Kale

My memories are that my mother used to make this dish when it was snowing – it is thin like a soup and served with a little olive oil and it makes you warm all the way through, which was perfect for those cold days in the Tuscan countryside.

Serves 6

3 bunches kale

800g polenta (cornmeal flour)

2 garlic cloves, peeled
  and finely chopped

160ml extra virgin olive oil,
  plus extra to serve

200g Parmesan cheese,
  grated, plus extra to serve

salt, to taste

Clean the kale, discarding the hard parts. Wash it repeatedly under running water and cut it into small strips. In a large casserole, bring about 2 litres of salted water to the boil. Add the kale and, while the water is still boiling, trickle in the polenta like light rain, stirring continuously with a metal whisk until all the polenta is added and you have a thick porridge. Continue cooking at a constant temperature (ideally you should use a flame-diffuser net), stirring now and then with a wooden spoon. Try to avoid scraping the bottom of the casserole.

After 40 minutes, add the chopped garlic and taste for seasoning, taking care not to burn yourself as the polenta will be very hot at this stage. Once the polenta is ready (in this case the polenta will have a slightly more liquid consistency than usual), whisk in the olive oil and Parmesan. Serve hot with a sprinkle of additional olive oil and more Parmesan to taste.

Zuppa di Cipolle all'Italiana
Italian-style Onion Soup

This onion soup is pale in colour, not dark like the French version, and uses lard to give the sharp, tangy taste (it is pancetta without the meat part!). This was another wonderful way for my family to cut down on wastage and use everything the scarce winter months had to offer.

Serves 6

500g large onions, peeled and sliced
100g lard, chopped
2 litres beef stock
300g white bread, toasted and cubed
60g Fontina cheese, grated
50g Parmesan cheese, grated
3 eggs, beaten

Place the onions and lard in a saucepan, heat gently and cook until the mixture starts to colour, then pour in the beef stock. Cook for a further 15 minutes.

Place the toasted cubes of bread in the bottoms of the soup bowls. Sprinkle in the Fontina and Parmesan and pour the beaten eggs over. Pour in the soup and serve.

Zuppa di Pomodoro al Timo
Golden Tomato Soup with Thyme

The secret of making sure we had delicious tomato soup throughout the winter was to dry the ripe, summer tomatoes so that we could add them to sauce when they were no longer in season. My grandmother would hang them on their vines, where they'd shrivel but never fall, until well into January or February. Nowadays, we can get tomatoes all year round, so to create an authentic feel, this recipe bakes fresh tomatoes first, to get some of the same intense flavours.

Serves 4

1.8kg tomatoes, quartered
5 garlic cloves, unpeeled
2 tbsp soft brown sugar
2 tbsp balsamic vinegar,
  plus extra to serve
6 sprigs thyme, leaves picked
900ml vegetable stock
salt and freshly ground black pepper,
  to taste

Preheat the oven to 150°C/Gas 2. Put the tomatoes and garlic on a baking tray. Sprinkle with the sugar, balsamic vinegar and thyme leaves. Roast the dressed tomatoes and garlic in the preheated oven for 1$\frac{1}{2}$ hours. Remove the tray from the oven, peel the garlic (take care as it will be hot!) and place it in a blender or food processor to purée with the tomatoes, thyme and any juices.

Pour the tomato and garlic purée into a saucepan and add the vegetable stock. Heat gently and season with salt, pepper and a little extra balsamic vinegar.

Petto d'Anatra al Fegato Grasso
Duck Breasts Stuffed with Foie Gras

This is another dish that I learned to make while I was at cookery school in Lausanne, Switzerland. Duck is a wonderful meat for winter dishes, because it is rich and dark and earthy to taste – especially when it's combined with succulent foie gras.

Serves 4

2 large duck breasts, skin on, approximately 900g total weight
160g foie gras, fat removed and reserved
1/2 tbsp black peppercorns
1 large onion, peeled and finely chopped
750g potatoes, peeled and chopped
1 small black truffle, grated
salt and freshly ground black pepper, to taste

Cut and open the duck breasts out flat (like a book) and season with salt. Cover with a layer of the foie gras and some peppercorns, then fold the breasts back together and seal with a toothpick. Make a few shallow cuts on the skin side.

Melt the foie gras fat in a casserole, add the onion and the potatoes and fry gently for 25 minutes. Add the duck breasts to the casserole (skin side down), and the grated truffle and season with salt and pepper. Increase the heat to high and cook the duck breasts for approximately 8 minutes on each side (or longer for a less pink meat). Transfer to a serving dish and serve immediately while very hot. If you wish, you can slice the duck breast before serving.

Trippa a Insalata
Tripe Salad

When I was growing up, tripe stalls were like the hot-dog stands we have today – you would find them on street corners (there was always one outside our local cinema), providing warm snacks for passers by. Prepare this salad an hour before serving to allow the flavours to mingle.

Serves 6

600g cooked tripe
2 carrots, peeled and finely chopped
1 celery stick, chopped
1 large red onion, peeled and
  finely chopped
2 garlic cloves, peeled and finely
  chopped
1 bunch of parsley, finely chopped
2 tbsp red wine vinegar
200ml extra virgin olive oil
1 dried red chilli, chopped (optional)
salt and freshly ground black pepper,
  to taste

Cut the tripe into strips, half of them about 1cm long and half about 5cm long. Place all the ingredients into a bowl, mix thoroughly and season. Sprinkle with some ground pepper and, if you like a spicy flavour, add some chopped chilli.

Fagiano all'Arancia
Pheasant with Orange Sauce

When I think of my father, I think of a man who, when he wasn't working, was always singing. He had a wonderful voice! He was also a wonderful cook, and often combined the two. He made this dish using pheasant he caught on our own farm during the winter months – we might even have it at Christmas with a glass of Nipozzano or Tignanello, delicious red Tuscan wines.

Serves 4

1 pheasant, approximately 800g
1 orange, plus extra slices to serve
2 sprigs rosemary
1/2 tbsp black peppercorns
150g sliced pancetta
40g lard
1 spring onion, trimmed and chopped
1 glass dry white wine
knob of butter
1 apple, peeled, cored and chopped
a pinch of sugar
1 tsp balsamic vinegar
salt and freshly ground black pepper,
    to taste

Preheat the oven to 200°C/Gas 6. Singe the bird if there are any remaining feather stumps. Then wash it and pat it dry with kitchen paper. Peel the orange and insert half the peel into the bird's cavity with one sprig of rosemary, the peppercorns, and the slices of pancetta (if there are too many to go inside the bird, you can wrap the remaining slices around the outside). Season inside and out with salt and pepper, then tie the pheasant up with cook's string.

Melt the lard in a casserole, add the spring onion, the remaining rosemary sprig and the remaining orange peel and sauté for 10 minutes. Add the pheasant, allow to brown on all sides over a high heat and pour in the wine to moisten. Cover and transfer the casserole to the preheated oven. After approximately 45 minutes, remove the lid from the casserole and continue cooking in the oven for a further 15 minutes, until the pheasant is cooked through. Remove the casserole from the oven, strain the cooking juices and set aside.

To make the sauce, cut the peeled orange into chunks. Melt the butter in a saucepan, add the orange chunks and apple and sauté gently for 5 minutes. Sprinkle with sugar and keep moist by adding the strained cooking juice from the pheasant, and the balsamic vinegar. Allow the sauce to reduce, then remove it from the heat and use a hand-held blender to process until smooth. Place the pheasant in the middle of a serving dish and pour around the fruit sauce. Decorate with slices of orange.

Arista alla Fiorentina
Florentine Roast Loin of Pork

Arista is a traditional Tuscan roast pork, in which garlic and fresh rosemary are poked inside the meat before cooking to give flavour throughout. Sometimes my mother would use winter wild boar instead of pork, and occasionally she would buy it ready-seasoned from the delicatessen.

Serves 8

1.5kg loin of pork, with the bone, skin removed
2 garlic cloves, peeled and finely chopped
1 tbsp chopped rosemary
salt and freshly ground black pepper, to taste

Preheat the oven to 180°C/Gas 4. Ask your butcher to detach the meat from the bone or to cut the bone in several places, to make slicing the cooked meat easier. If the meat has been detached from the bone, ask the butcher to give it to you and then tie the bone and meat together to add extra flavour during cooking. Your butcher should also be able to remove the skin for you.

Mix the garlic with the rosemary, salt and pepper. Pierce the meat with a sharp, thin-bladed knife and insert the garlic mixture in the holes. Place the meat in an ovenproof dish and season with plenty of salt and pepper. Roast in the oven for 35 minutes, basting regularly with the meat's own juices. After 35 minutes, test the meat with a fork; it's done when the fork goes in easily.

Cook's tip: If you're planning to serve the pork with roast potatoes, cut the potatoes into pieces and cook them in the meat juice.

Palline di Carne al Sugo
Meatballs with Tomato Sauce

We used to eat meatballs as a *secondo piatto* – a main course – not as an accompaniment to the *primo* pasta course as you might expect. Once we'd finished our pasta, my mother would leave our bowls on the table, with the tomato sauce that was left in the bottoms, and then serve us the meatballs. We dipped them into the leftover sauce and ate them up just like that. In this version, you make the sauce to go with the meatballs. Serve it with short, ridged pasta, too, if you wish.

Serves 4

400g minced beef
zest of 1 lemon
flour, for dusting
2 tbsp extra virgin olive oil
30g butter
1 garlic clove, peeled and
  slightly crushed
150ml dry white wine
500g tomatoes, peeled (see p.59)
1 handful of basil leaves, torn
salt and freshly ground black pepper,
  to taste

Put the beef in a bowl with the lemon zest and a pinch of salt. Moisten your hands with water and slowly mix together – squeeze a handful at a time, forcing the meat between your fingers. Form the meat into balls the size of walnuts and dredge them lightly in flour.

Heat the oil and butter in a saucepan. Add the garlic clove and sauté until lightly browned. Remove the garlic from the pan and add the meatballs. Sauté them until they, too, are browned, and as they cook, sprinkle them with the wine. As soon as the wine has evaporated, add the tomatoes and break them up with a fork. Season with salt and pepper. Cover the saucepan and cook over a moderate heat for about 15 minutes. Add the basil leaves, stir and serve.

Stufato di Vitello con Funghi e Mascarpone
Veal Stew with Mushrooms and Mascarpone

My sister still lives in Tuscany, close to where we grew up, and often when I go home she makes this for me – a reminder of the wonderful stew, with its fantastically creamy sauce, that our mother used to make. You can add any winter vegetables, but mushrooms are my favourites.

Serves 6

butter, for frying

300g onions, peeled and finely sliced

800g veal fillet, diced

10g dried mushrooms, soaked in boiling-hot water for 30 minutes, then drained and sliced

50g walnuts, chopped

2 glasses dry white wine

vegetable stock (enough to cover the meat)

300g champignon mushrooms, roughly chopped

2 tbsp finely chopped parsley

150g mascarpone

salt and freshly ground black pepper, to taste

Melt a large knob of butter in a large frying pan, add the onions and fry gently for a few minutes. Add the meat and cook until it is browned on all sides. Then, add the soaked mushrooms, 35g of the walnuts, the wine and sufficient vegetable stock to cover the meat. Season with salt and pepper, cover and simmer for approximately 1$\frac{1}{2}$ hours.

Meanwhile, in a separate saucepan melt another knob of butter. Add the champignon mushrooms and sauté on a high heat, until soft and cooked through. Add the parsley and season with salt and pepper. Remove from the heat, set aside and keep warm.

Once the meat is cooked, using a slotted spoon remove it from the saucepan and set aside. Allow the juice left in the pan to reduce a little. Stir in the mascarpone and cook for a few minutes. Season with salt and pepper and whisk to combine the sauce. Place the meat on a serving dish and pour the sauce over. Garnish with the remaining walnuts and top with the sautéed mushrooms.

Portafogli di Vitello Impanati e Fritti
Stuffed Veal Escalopes

I remember this dish being made quite often at our house. We used to have it on a Sunday as a main course and my mother would serve it with piles of winter vegetables. Veal wasn't the rare or expensive meat we think of today, although it was special.

Serves 4

extra virgin olive oil, for frying

30g diced pancetta

70g leek, sliced

200g courgettes, sliced

80g red chicory (radicchio),
  sliced lengthways

2 tbsp grated Parmesan cheese

a pinch of grated nutmeg

4 veal cutlets with bone,
  each cutlet approximately 300g

12 slices of white bread,
  made into breadcrumbs

finely chopped mixed herbs
  (sage, thyme, rosemary)

flour, for dusting

3 eggs, beaten

butter, for frying

salt and freshly ground black pepper,
  to taste

To make the stuffing, heat a little oil in a frying pan, add the pancetta and fry gently. Add the leek and courgettes and, after a few minutes, the red chicory. Wait for the red chicory to soften, then season with salt and pepper and transfer to a bowl. Stir in the Parmesan and nutmeg. Divide this mixture in four portions.

Slice and open out (like a book) the veal cutlets and flatten them. Season with salt and pepper and spread each cutlet with a portion of stuffing. Close the cutlets by pressing the edges with the flat surface of a knife blade to make dents all along, forming four veal parcels. Mix the breadcrumbs and herbs together. Roll the cutlets in flour, dip them into the beaten egg and coat with the herby breadcrumbs.

Melt the butter in a frying pan, add the cutlets and fry for 4–5 minutes on each side, adding more butter if necessary to prevent the cutlets burning. Serve the cutlets hot with your choice of vegetables.

Fagioli con Salsiccie

Beans and Sausage

This is the perfect winter dish – it's a hearty, warming one-pot meal, with all the vegetables and meat mixed in together. It is best made with proper, rich, meaty Italian pork sausages, which are small and fat. However, if you can't get them, use best-quality, butcher-bought regular pork sausages and twist each in the middle to make two smaller, fatter ones.

Serves 4

8 small Italian pork sausages
2 tbsp extra virgin olive oil
1 garlic clove, peeled and squashed
3–4 sage leaves
250g cannellini beans, tinned or fresh
salt, to taste

Using a fork, prick the sausages and put them in a bowl of boiling water for a few minutes. Drain and set aside.

Heat the oil in a casserole, add the garlic and sage and lightly fry for a minute or so. Add the beans and the sausages and cook for about 5 minutes over a low heat, or until the sausages are cooked through. Season with salt and serve hot.

Medaglioni di Bottatrice al Limone
Medallions of Monkfish in Lemon

Today, monkfish is an expensive fish to buy, but when I was growing up it was so abundant in the seas off the coast of Tuscany that fishermen used to throw it away! This meant that if you wanted a good, meaty fish dish, monkfish was a relatively inexpensive option to fit the bill. Monkfish makes a good winter fish, because it is heavier and meatier than other types.

Serves 4

1 monkfish fillet, approximately 500g
flour, for dusting
3 egg yolks, beaten
50g butter, plus extra for frying
juice of 1 lemon
1 bunch of parsley, finely chopped
salt and freshly ground pink pepper
2 beef tomatoes, thickly sliced, to serve

Cut the monkfish fillet into 12 equal slices (medallions), sprinkle them with salt and flour, then dip them in the beaten yolks.

Melt some butter in a frying pan, add the fish and fry on both sides until golden. (Add more butter after frying each batch of medallions to avoid overheating.) When the medallions are cooked, drain them on kitchen paper, and keep them warm.

Meanwhile, heat the 50g of butter in a small saucepan, add the lemon juice, parsley, a pinch of salt and a generous sprinkling of pink pepper. Place the medallions on individual serving plates and pour the sauce over. Serve with slices of the beef tomato separating the medallions.

Polenta e Baccalá
Polenta with Salt Cod

I think it's perfectly possible that this delicious fish dish was the most popular dish in the whole of Tuscany! My mother made it for my father and me very often, because we loved it so much. *Baccalá* is preserved cod, so it makes a good winter staple. This recipe uses *bramata*, which is a very fine cornmeal flour, available in the home-baking department of most good supermarkets.

Serves 6

800g *baccalá* (salt cod)
wheat flour (type '00'), for coating
extra virgin olive oil, for frying
butter, for frying

For the polenta
1 tbsp coarse salt
400g cornmeal flour
200g *bramata* cornmeal flour

For the sauce
butter, for frying
1 celery stick, finely chopped
1/2 small onion, peeled and
  finely chopped
1 carrot, peeled and finely chopped
1/2 garlic clove, peeled and
  finely chopped
200g parsley, finely chopped
1 tbsp pickled capers, finely chopped
4 unsalted anchovy fillets, finely chopped
1 glass dry white wine
flour (optional)
salt and freshly ground black pepper,
  to taste

Soak the cod under a slow-running tap for 24 hours. Drain the cod, pat it dry and cut it into strips along the length of the fillet. Coat the strips in the flour.

To cook the polenta, add the salt to a saucepan containing 2 litres of water. Bring the water almost to the boil, then trickle in the two flours like light rain, stirring continuously with a wooden spoon. Keep stirring until the mixture reaches boiling point, then reduce the heat to medium-low and cook, uncovered, for about 2 hours, stirring from time to time.

Meanwhile, fry the cod slices in olive oil and butter, turning them until golden on both sides. Drain them on kitchen paper, and set aside.

To make the sauce, in a separate saucepan melt a knob of butter and sauté all the vegetables with the garlic, parsley, capers and anchovies for a few minutes. Add the fried cod strips and the wine. Once the wine has evaporated, add enough hot water to obtain sufficient sauce to cover the fish (if necessary, add some flour to thicken the cooking juices). Keep warm until the polenta is cooked.

Place the polenta and the fish in separate serving dishes. Serve the polenta very hot and the cod with plenty of sauce.

Tortino di Salmone e Radicchio Rosso
Salmon and Red Chicory Tartlets

This recipe is one of my own creations. I invented it after I arrived in the UK, which (believe it or not) was where I ate salmon for the very first time. Red chicory is a winter vegetable and I added it into this dish to give some moisture to the salmon, which I think can be quite dry.

Serves 4

butter, for frying
400g red chicory (radicchio),
   cut into strips
1 garlic clove, peeled and chopped
600g salmon fillet, thinly sliced
3 tbsp fish stock
1 spring onion, trimmed and chopped
3 tbsp dry white wine
1/2 tsp curry powder
salt and freshly ground black pepper,
   to taste

Preheat the oven to 190°C/Gas 5. Melt a knob of butter in a casserole, add the red chicory and garlic, and season with a pinch of salt and some pepper, and sauté for a few minutes. Divide the chicory and the salmon in four equal portions and set aside.

To make the tartlets, line a baking tray with butter and baking parchment. Place a pastry cutter with a 12cm diameter on top. Inside the pastry cutter, make a first layer with some salmon slices, then a second layer with some red chicory strips and so on, alternating the layers and seasoning with salt and pepper between layers until you've completed one portion. Repeat to make three more tartlets. Sprinkle the tartlets with fish stock and cook in the preheated oven for approximately 12 minutes.

Meanwhile, melt another knob of butter in a saucepan, add the spring onion and sauté gently, then add the wine, a pinch of salt and the curry powder and reduce the sauce until it has the consistency of single cream.

Place the hot tartlets on individual serving plates and pour over the sauce to serve.

Torta di Pere e Fichi
Pear and Fig Tart

Even when fresh vegetables were scarce during the winter months, there was always an abundance of fruit in our house. This meant that there were always fruit cakes, tarts and biscuits. I would take a slice of this pear and fig tart to school as a snack – and it was so delicious, all my friends wanted some, too!

Serves 6–8

200g shortcrust pastry
flour, for dusting
6 pears, peeled, cored and halved
   lengthways
4 dried figs, quartered
1 tbsp ground cinnamon
150g butter
150ml honey
icing sugar, to decorate
ice cream or single cream, to serve

Preheat the oven to 220°C/Gas 7. Dust a board with the flour and roll out the pastry to line a 25cm tart tin. Arrange the pear halves around the edge of the tart and the slices of fig in the middle. Sprinkle over the cinnamon. Melt the butter and honey together in a small saucepan, then, using a brush, spread the honey mixture over the fruit.

Bake in the preheated oven for 10 minutes, then reduce the temperature to 200°C/Gas 6 and bake for a further 15 minutes. Remove from the oven, dust generously with icing sugar and serve hot with vanilla ice cream or a drizzle of single cream.

Variation: If you prefer, you can make individual tartlets. Using the pastry, cut out 4–6 circles, each 15cm in diameter. Thinly slice the peeled, cored pears and the dried figs and place alternating pear and fig slices in a fan shape on the pastry circles, sprinkling with cinnamon as you go. Brush over the butter and honey as before, and bake at 220°C for 5 minutes, then at 200°C for a further 10 minutes.

Torta di Riso
Sweet Risotto Cake

A sweet cake made with risotto rice, this is a famous Florentine dish that the city-dwellers would tuck into with their morning cappuccino. However, it also makes a wonderful dessert – a sort of tangy rice pudding that's thick enough to slice.

Serves 6–8

150g shortgrain risotto rice
1.25 litres whole milk
butter, for greasing
2 tbsp semolina, for dusting
8 eggs
250g caster sugar
3 tbsp brandy
grated zest or juice of ½ lemon

Preheat the oven to 180°C/Gas 4. Place the rice and two-thirds (a little under 900ml) of the milk in a saucepan, bring to the boil, then reduce the heat to low and simmer for 10 minutes, then drain.

Butter a 25cm cake tin thoroughly (do not use a loose-bottomed tin or all the liquid will ooze away) and dust with the semolina. Turn the cake tin upside down to remove any loose semolina.

Beat the eggs in a large bowl until foaming and pale yellow. Gradually add the sugar, brandy and the lemon zest or juice. Stir thoroughly, add the drained rice and the remaining milk. Pour the mixture into the cake tin and bake for about 50 minutes or until a skewer inserted in the centre comes out clean. The cake should be well set and golden brown. Serve warm or cold.

Composta di Frutta Secca
Dried Fruit Compote

Dried fruit compotes lasted all winter, providing fruit for my family in even the coldest frosts. The addition of the nuts and cinnamon to this dish gives a warming feel that so reminds me of those cold winter afternoons.

Serves 4–5

250g dried Agen prunes
150g dried apricots
100g dried figs
200ml white wine
60g sugar
1 tsp ground cinnamon
20g flaked almonds, to decorate
100g chopped walnuts, to decorate

Preheat the oven to 170°C/Gas 3. Place the prunes, apricots and figs in an ovenproof dish. Add 150ml water and the white wine and place in the oven for 10 minutes. Then, stir in the sugar and return to the oven for a further 10 minutes. After that, add the cinnamon and cook for a final 5 minutes.

While still warm, transfer the compote to individual dishes and decorate with the flaked almonds and the walnuts.

Torta della Nonna
Grandma's Pie

If you want to eat an authentic Italian cake, this has to be it. Every *nonna*, up and down Italy, makes this pie at Christmas time or at Epiphany (on 6 January) for the whole family to enjoy. It's the ultimate Italian celebration cake.

Serves 6–8

For the paste
500g plain flour
300g butter
200g sugar
4 eggs
zest of ½ lemon
1 tbsp vanilla extract
a pinch of salt

For the filling
500ml whole milk
1 vanilla pod, cut lengthways
  to release the flavour
4 eggs
100g sugar
60g plain flour
60g pine nuts
icing sugar, to serve

To make the paste, sieve the flour into a large bowl and make a well in the centre. Add the butter, sugar, eggs, lemon zest, vanilla extract and salt into the well. Mix slowly, gradually bringing the flour to the centre to combine the ingredients together. Once combined, put the paste in the refrigerator and let it rest for 3 hours.

Preheat the oven to 200°C/Gas 6. To make the filling, boil the milk in a saucepan with the vanilla pod. Beat three of the eggs in a large bowl, then add the sugar and flour and combine. Add the hot milk, discarding the vanilla pod, and stir to combine again. Return the mixture to the saucepan and bring to the boil.

Roll out the refrigerated sweet paste to line a 25cm pie dish, leaving enough to make a 'lid', too. Once the filling has cooled down, pour it into the casing so that the casing is two-thirds full. Sprinkle over half the pine nuts, then cover with another layer of sweet paste to make a lid on the pie.

Separate the yolk of the remaining egg and whisk it. Using a pastry brush, brush the egg yolk over the pie before sprinkling over the remaining pine nuts. Cook the pie in the preheated oven for 35 minutes. Serve hot or cold, generously sprinkled with icing sugar.

Wine and Food

A long time ago on my family's lands in Vinci we had whole fields dedicated to vine-growing. During the grape harvest we would pick the grapes by hand and crush them with our feet – just like you see in the movies! Today, in Italy, making wine is too expensive unless you dedicate yourself to its production, with a specialist winemaker on site to guide you through the science of creating something beautiful for people to drink. As a result, these days my family's vineyards have given way to olive groves, which are much easier to manage. Instead, for La Famiglia, I import my wine from Italy, some from Tuscany, but also from other parts of the country, so that I have something to suit all the dishes on my menu.

There's nothing particularly complicated about the way in which I encourage my diners to match their food and wine, but some of the advice I give may be a little surprising. First, to be authentically Tuscan, I encourage my diners to drink mostly red wine – even with foods that you might instinctively think would match best with whites. This is because, in Tuscany, if not most of Italy except for the very north, the best wine is red.

However, like most things in life, not all reds were created equal, and although it may seem strange to match red to light foods, some, such as the region's famous Chianti, made from Sangiovese grapes, are perfect for drinking with light dishes, such as light pastas or even with fish. Chianti, particularly Chianti Classico, from the centre of the Chianti-producing region, is fresh, fruity and easy on the palate. To eat a heavy dish with such a lively wine would be to overpower the wine altogether, to lose its freshness.

Although I insist upon Italian wine in the restaurant, I am not dogmatic about it coming from Tuscany. Indeed, many other regions of Italy produce wonderful reds that suit the light dishes on my menu. The Veneto (which stretches from Venice westwards to Verona) gives us Bardolino, from vines grown on the hillsides surrounding Lake Garda. The wine is a blend of Corvina, Rondinella and Molinara grapes and makes wonderfully easy drinking that's perfect to accompany fish or light meats. Meanwhile Piemonte, in the northwest of Italy, produces Dolcetto d'Alba. This smooth wine goes perfectly with Tuscan cured meats or truffle-based dishes.

Of course, if you prefer to drink white wine, I suggest a wine made from Pinot Grigio grapes, perhaps from Collio, Alto Adige or the Veneto, all in the northeast of Italy. This crisp, white wine is best served well chilled and is a good match for fish and shellfish dishes and for dishes with mushrooms or even poultry.

For a bolder, fuller wine to drink with heavier dishes, such as wild boar and beef, one of my favourites is Brunello di Montalcino. This wine comes from grapes grown on the gentle hills immediately south of the main Chianti-producing region of Tuscany. It is aged for more than three years in wood and is rich, robust and proud and has great longevity. Alternatively, you can try Vino Nobile di Montepulciano. Like a richer, deeper version of a Chianti, this wine goes well with dishes such as Florentine beef stew. However, some of the best Italian full-bodied red wine now comes from the very south of the country. Puglia, which lies in Italy's heel, is home to wines such as Salice Selentino and Levarano, made with the Negroamaro grape variety. These are robust and inky-deep, and delicious with herby, meaty dishes such as pasta with wild boar sauce (see p.194).

One of Tuscany's most famous wine exports is Vin Santo. Made from grapes that are left to hang on the vines until Easter (hence the name *santo*, meaning 'holy') to concentrate the sugars, Vin Santo is an intensely sweet wine that is aged in small wooden barrels for at least five years, giving a deep golden colour. Vin Santo matches perfectly with sweet desserts – however, if you want to drink it like a true Tuscan, try it after dessert, dunked with *cantucci* biscuits (see p.173).

Maccioni Olive Oil

Olive oil is very much like wine. Year to year, the climate, the soil, the winds and water and the way the plants are tended, can all affect the fruit of the olive tree, giving rise to subtle but noticeable distinctions between the kinds of oil an olive estate will produce. One year the oil might be softer with a smooth, rich flavour, while the following year it might be *piccante* – spicy – and a little more deep. Equally, just as the winemaker must know exactly when to pick the grapes to produce just the right quality of wine, so the maker of olive oil must choose just the right time to harvest his olives – in autumn, while the fruit are still mostly green, but in places just beginning to turn black is perfect for me.

Also rather like wine – with its various grape varieties – olive oil is made from different varieties of olives. In Tuscany there are five types of olive, but the three main varieties are Muraiolo, Leccino and Mignolino. I think the best oil comes from a blend of Muraiolo with a little Leccino – it is deep and flavourful, and rich in colour with a nutty, herby taste.

At La Famiglia, I use only the finest quality olive oil from the olive groves now run by my cousin Pietro. These olives are tended with the greatest care and, in autumn, when the fruit are ripe, they are hand picked during the day. Once the olives are picked from the trees, they are dropped into a net and then the stalks, stems and leaves are removed by hand before the fruit is taken to the mill for pressing. On the same day as picking, the olives are washed, then placed on large, circular stone wheels, where they are milled into a paste. If you leave olives for more than 24 hours between picking and milling, the resulting oil will acquire unwanted acidity – the whole process has to be completed in a day, so that the oil is fresh, smooth and delicious.

The olive paste is then pressed to extract the juice from the fruit. At this stage, the liquid is not pure oil, but a mixture of oil and water. Traditionally, the two are separated by the simple act of gravity – oil is lighter than water, so it floats, then the water can be drained away from the bottom of the container. However, today most presses use centrifugal force, spinning the water–oil mixture to separate the two. This is more precise and reduces the risk that water will be left with the oil during bottling, which can sometimes cause the oil to degrade.

The first pressing of the olives produces 'virgin' olive oil – the name 'extra virgin' is given only to oil from this pressing that meets certain standards of chemical make up. A second pressing may ensue, which produces regular standard oil.

There is nothing more wonderful than dipping a hunk of fresh ciabatta into freshly pressed olive oil. I used to do just that as a child – even before the oil had been removed for bottling. Now, I insist that the olive oil from those very same olive groves is the only oil used in the cooking in my restaurant. It arrives directly from my cousin and, each year, I can't wait to open the first bottle and taste what that year's harvest has brought. Smooth or *piccante*, it is always beautiful – and it is a very precise and welcome reminder of my home.

Conversion Charts

All the recipes in this book use metric measurements. The following tables provide conversions from metric to imperial and US cups, as relevant. Never mix measurement systems – use the same system of conversion throughout in order to ensure the quantities relative to one another remain the same.

Weight

Metric	Imperial	Metric	Imperial
6g	$1/8$oz	280g	10oz
10g	$1/4$oz	300g	$10^{1/2}$oz
15g	$1/2$oz	320g	$11^{1/4}$oz
20g	$3/4$oz	325g	$11^{1/2}$oz
25g/30g	1oz	350g	12oz
35g	$1^{1/4}$oz	360g	$12^{3/4}$oz
40g	$1^{1/2}$oz	375g	13oz
50g	$1^{3/4}$oz	400g	14oz
55g	2oz	425g	15oz
60g	$2^{1/4}$oz	450g	1lb
70g/75g	$2^{1/2}$oz	500g	1lb 2oz
80g	$2^{3/4}$oz	550g	1lb 4oz
90g	$3^{1/4}$oz	600g	1lb 5oz
100g	$3^{1/2}$oz	650g	1lb 7oz
120g	$4^{1/4}$oz	700g	1lb 9oz
125g	$4^{1/2}$oz	750g	1lb 10oz
130g	$4^{3/4}$oz	800g	1lb 12oz
140g	5oz	850g	1lb 14oz
150g	$5^{1/2}$oz	900g	2lb
160g	$5^{3/4}$oz	950g	2lb 2oz
175g	6oz	1kg	2lb 4oz
200g	7oz	1.2kg	2lb 12oz
225g	8oz	1.3kg	3lb
250g	9oz	1.5kg	3lb 5oz
275g	$9^{3/4}$oz	2kg	4lb 8oz

Volume

Metric	Imperial	US tbsp/cups
5ml	—	1 tsp
15/20ml	$1/2$fl oz	1 tbsp
30ml	1fl oz	2 tbsp
60ml	2fl oz	4 tbsp
75ml	$2^{1/4}$fl oz	4 tbsp + 1 tsp
80ml	$2^{1/2}$fl oz	5 tbsp
85ml	$2^{3/4}$fl oz	5 tbsp + 1 tsp
90ml	3fl oz	6 tbsp
100ml	$3^{1/2}$fl oz	7 tbsp
120ml	$3^{3/4}$fl oz	scant $1/2$ cup
125ml	4fl oz	$1/2$ cup
150ml	5fl oz	$1/2$ cup + 2 tbsp
160ml	$5^{1/4}$fl oz	scant $2/3$ cup
165ml	$5^{1/2}$fl oz	$2/3$ cup
175ml	$5^{3/4}$fl oz	scant $3/4$ cup
185ml	6fl oz	$3/4$ cup
200ml	7fl oz	$3/4$ cup + 2 tbsp
220ml	$7^{1/2}$fl oz	scant 1 cup
225ml	$7^{3/4}$fl oz	scant 1 cup
240ml	8fl oz	1 cup
250ml	9fl oz	1 cup + 2 tbsp
300ml	$10^{1/2}$fl oz	$1^{1/4}$ cups + 1 tbsp
350ml	12fl oz	$1^{1/2}$ cups
400ml	$13^{1/2}$fl oz	$1^{3/4}$ cups
500ml	17fl oz	2 cups
600ml	21fl oz	$2^{1/2}$ cups + 2 tbsp
750ml	26fl oz	$3^{1/4}$ cups
900ml	31fl oz	$3^{3/4}$ cups + 2 tbsp
1 litre	35fl oz	$4^{1/3}$ cups
1.2 litres	40fl oz	5 cups
1.25 litres	44fl oz	$5^{1/2}$ cups
1.5 litres	52fl oz	$6^{1/2}$ cups
2 litres	70fl oz	$8^{3/4}$ cups

Glossary of Terms

Length

Metric	Imperial
1.5mm	less than $^1/_{16}$in
3mm	$^1/_8$in
1cm	$^1/_4$in
1.5cm	$^5/_8$in
2cm	$^3/_4$in
2.5cm	1in
3cm	$1^1/_4$in
4cm	$1^1/_2$in
5cm	2in
6cm	$2^1/_2$in
9cm	$3^1/_2$in
10cm	4in
20cm	8in
25cm	10in
28cm	$11^1/_4$in
30cm	12in

Temperature

°C	°F	Gas
85	185	—
100	200	$^1/_2$
110	225	$^1/_2$
130	250	1
150	300	2
160	315	2–3
170	325	3
180	350	4
190	375	5
200	400	6
220	425	7

The following is a list of the UK food names and cooking terms that appear in this book and are known by an alternative name in the USA.

UK	USA
aubergine	eggplant
bottled	jarred
broad bean	fava bean
clingfilm	plastic wrap
courgette	zucchini
dark chocolate	bittersweet chocolate
demerara sugar	raw sugar
digestive biscuits	graham crackers
double cream	heavy cream
flaked almonds	sliced almonds
frying pan	skillet
greaseproof paper	wax paper
grill (noun)	broiler
grill (verb)	broil
icing sugar	powdered sugar
minced meat	ground meat
plain chocolate	semi-sweet chocolate
plain flour	all-purpose flour
prawn	shrimp
red/green/yellow pepper	red/green/yellow bell pepper
rocket	arugula
self-raising flour	self-rising flour
sieve	strainer
single cream	light cream
spring onions	scallions
tomato purée	tomato paste
wholemeal	wholewheat

Index

Acknowledgements

Alvaro Maccioni would like to thank his chef Quinto Cecchetti and sous chef Sergio Miranda Paolo Lopez, as well as his restaurant manager Gennaro Manna. Furthermore, his thanks to David Loftus for taking the beautiful photographs in this book.

The Publisher would like to acknowledge and thank Vivien James for early editorial participation, and Brian Stone, for his support and enthusiasm on this project.

Picture Credits

The Publisher would like to thank the following photographers and picture agency for their kind permission to reproduce the following photographs in this book:

pp.4–5: Olive farms on the hillsides around Vinci, Tuscany (© Ted Spiegel/Corbis).
pp. 27, 28–9: A springtime view of the Orcia Valley in Tuscany (© Fabio Muzzi/Cultura/Corbis).
pp.77, 78–9: Mist covers the Tuscan countryside (© Frank Krahmer/Corbis).
pp.128: Ancient olive trees near Sant'Antimo, Tuscany (© Hubert Stadler/Corbis).
pp.129, 130–31: Vineyards in the Chianti Classico region of Tuscany, in Autumn (© Fabio Muzzi/Cultura/Corbis).
p.179, 180–81: Panzano, Chianti, Tuscany, during the winter snow (© Atlantide Phototravel/Corbis).
pp.228–9: Tuscan hills at dawn (© Angelo Cavalli/Corbis).

Commissioned photography not by David Loftus:
pp.9, 10 & 16: Photographs by Luke Hayes from Alvaro Maccioni's family archive © Palazzo Editions Ltd.
pp.229 & 231: Photographs by Luke Hayes © Palazzo Editions Ltd.

All other archive photographs: © David Loftus.

Jacket credits
Jacket design: Bernard Higton
Back cover photograph: David Loftus
Author photograph: Luke Hayes
Line artwork (jacket and endpapers): Zoe More O'Ferrall